Own the Digital Space:
Your 2024 Brand Marketing Playbook

Ayham Ramadan

Copyright © 2024 Ayham Ramadan

All rights reserved.

ISBN: 9798325103308

"Dedicated to the visionary leaders who have fueled my journey over the past two decades. Your mentorship, guidance, and unwavering belief in my potential have propelled me to new heights of expertise and performance. Thank you for shaping my path and inspiring me to own the digital space.".

CONTENTS

	Acknowledgments	i
1	The Brand World Today	1
2	Your Brand's Voice and Look	15
3	Building Together: Creating a Community	26
4	Making Stories that Stick	32
5	Video Dominance: Formats and Strategies	39
6	Dive In: AR, VR, and Your Brand	46
7	Social Media Pro Moves	48
8	Making Friends: Smart Partnerships	52
9	PR in the Digital Age	57
10	Tracking and Feeling the Vibes	62
11	Doing the Right Thing	69
12	Marketing Trends to Watch in 2025 & Beyond	74

ACKNOWLEDGMENTS

"To the daring entrepreneurs around the globe who are fearlessly reshaping industries and challenging the status quo: Your boundless creativity, relentless pursuit of innovation, and unwavering determination to succeed inspire us all. With each groundbreaking idea and bold endeavor, you raise the bar of human potential and redefine what is possible. Thank you for igniting the spark of possibility and driving us toward a future filled with limitless opportunities."

THE BRAND WORLD TODAY

1. Brief overview of how consumer expectations have shifted.

Values over price: Increasingly, consumers (especially those in younger demographics) are willing to pay more or choose a brand with aligned values even if a cheaper competitor exists. They want to feel good about where their money is going.

Showcases:
- **Patagonia:** This outdoor apparel company is known for its commitment to environmentalism, repair programs, and activism. They command a premium price, but have an incredibly loyal customer base due to aligning with the values of conscious consumers.
- **Everlane:** This clothing brand prioritizes radical transparency, sharing details on their factories, pricing, and materials. While not the cheapest option, they attract customers who value knowing where their clothes come from and under what conditions they were made.
- **TOMS:** The "one for one" shoe company has built a social mission into its core. Consumers may pay slightly more knowing their purchase helps provide shoes for those in need.

Action, not just words: Consumers are savvy to "performative activism" or "woke-washing". They want to see brands put their values into practice through concrete actions, partnerships, internal policies, and support for social causes.

Case Studies: Successes
- **Ben & Jerry's:** This ice cream company is known for its advocacy on social justice issues. They back up their messaging with donations, campaigns, and by incorporating activism into their flavors and marketing. Analyze their long-term success and how their actions have built brand loyalty.
- **Lush Cosmetics:** This brand's "Charity Pot" model donates 100% of the sales of a particular body lotion to grassroots charities. They also openly campaign against animal testing and for ethical sourcing. Highlight how their tangible actions have attracted a dedicated customer base.

Transparency as the baseline: Consumers now expect a higher level of transparency. They want to know where products are made, the brand's stance on social issues, the environmental impact of their choices, and how companies treat their employees.

Showcases:
- **Ingredient Transparency Apps:** Apps like Think Dirty or Skin Deep (EWG) allow users to scan product barcodes for information about ingredient safety and potential concerns. This empowers consumers to make informed choices, even at the store shelf.
- **Patagonia's Footprint Chronicles:** This section of their website tracks the environmental impact of specific products, including admitting where they fall short. This honesty has strengthened brand loyalty among eco-conscious consumers.
- **"Certified" Labels Gaining Importance:** Labels such as Fair Trade, USDA Organic, and non-GMO certifications are becoming more influential in purchasing decisions as consumers seek assurances beyond a brand's own claims.

The power of the individual: Social media has amplified the voice of the individual consumer. Dissatisfied consumers can quickly share their experiences and influence others, making brands highly accountable for their actions.

- **Social Media Impact**
    - **Wendy's "Nuggs for Carter":** In 2017, a teenager named Carter Wilkerson tweeted at Wendy's asking how many retweets he'd need for a year of free chicken nuggets. The tweet went viral, and Wendy's embraced the challenge. Carter broke the retweet record, Wendy's donated to charity, and this lighthearted campaign showcased the potential reach of a single consumer.
    - **Chewy's Customer Service:** Chewy, an online pet supplies retailer, is famous for acts of kindness towards individual customers. From sending flowers after a pet's passing to surprise gifts, stories of these interactions have been widely shared online, building immense brand loyalty.

- **Individuals Driving Change**
    - **Greta Thunberg:** This young climate activist is a prime example of how one person's voice can spark global movements. Her school strikes and speeches have forced the climate crisis to the forefront of political and corporate agendas.
    - **Fashion Revolution's "Who Made My Clothes?"** This social media campaign encourages consumers to tag brands, asking for transparency about production. It began with a small group concerned about sweatshops and now has global reach, pressuring major clothing companies to respond.
    - **Patagonia Lawsuit:** Yvon Chouinard, Patagonia's founder, donated the entire company to fight climate change. This radical act of individual decision demonstrates the power to use a business for large-scale good.

Community-minded buying: Consumers are increasingly looking to support brands that foster a sense of community, whether through shared values, exclusive experiences, or simply a focus on bringing people together.

- **Large Scale Initiatives:**
    - **The "15% Pledge":** This non-profit seeks to get major retailers to commit 15% of their shelf space to Black-owned businesses. It was started by a single founder, Aurora James, and gained significant traction. Major retailers like Sephora and Target are now onboard.
    - **Etsy's Uplift Initiative:** In 2020, Etsy pledged significant resources specifically to support Black-owned and underrepresented businesses on its platform. This includes funding grants, offering mentorship, and creating special promotions to drive traffic towards these shops.

- **Local and Individual Impact:**
    - **Farmers' Markets:** The classic example. Buying directly from farmers or local producers supports the regional economy and fosters a sense of community with the people behind your food.
    - **"Shop Local" Campaigns:** Many towns and cities have initiatives encouraging people to support locally-owned businesses over large chains. These campaigns showcase specials, create directories, and organize events.
    - **Community-Supported Agriculture (CSAs):** Subscriptions to a local farm offer direct support in exchange for a share of the harvest.
    - **Handmade/Artisanal Markets:** These events highlight local makers and give consumers a chance to put their money directly into the hands of creators within their community.

2. Data and statistics on consumer preference for brands with values.

General Preference for Values-Driven Companies:

- 83% of consumers want brands to align with their values. (5W Public Relations, 2022)
- 72% of consumers believe it's more important than ever for the companies they buy from to reflect their values. (Shelton Group's "Sustainability Pulse Check", 2022)
- 63% of consumers worldwide prefer to purchase from purpose-driven brands. (Accenture Strategy, 2018)
- 64% of consumers say they're likely to choose or avoid a brand solely because of its stand on a societal issue. (2020 Edelman Trust Barometer)

Willingness to Pay More:

- 66% of consumers are willing to pay more for products and services from companies committed to positive social and environmental impact. (Nielsen, 2015)
- 53% of consumers say they'd pay more for brands that are environmentally committed. (Shelton Group's "Sustainability Pulse Check", 2022)
- Impact on Purchasing Decisions:
- 91% of global consumers are likely to switch brands to one that supports a good cause, given similar price and quality. (Cone Communications CSR Study, 2017)
- 87% of consumers would purchase a product because a company advocates for an issue they care about. (Cone Communications CSR Study, 2017)
- Demographic Trends:

Millennials and Gen Z are especially values-driven: Multiple studies support that these generations are more likely to spend with ethical brands than older groups. (Sources: Cone Communications, GlobalWebIndex)

3. The rise of the discerning buyer

Who is the Discerning Buyer?
- **Informed:** They do their research. This extends beyond product specs to company ethics, social impact, environmental footprint, and labor practices.
- **Values-driven:** They want their spending to align with their beliefs. This includes avoiding brands that clash with their values, and seeking those actively making a positive impact.
- **Skeptical of Marketing:** They see through "greenwashing" or superficial woke-posturing. They demand authenticity and demonstrated action from brands.
- **Community-Minded:** They're influenced by peer reviews, online communities sharing experiences, and recommendations from those they trust.
- **Not Necessarily Wealthy:** Discerning buying is a mindset, not tied exclusively to income level. Even budget-conscious shoppers may prioritize spending with ethical businesses.

Why the Rise?
- **Access to Information:** The internet makes it easier to research companies, compare alternatives, and uncover controversies.
- **Awareness of Social/Environmental Issues:** Increased media coverage and online discussion highlights problems that discerning buyers want to help solve (or at least, not contribute further towards).
- **Distrust of Traditional Institutions:** Scandals and a sense that powerful entities often don't act in the public's interest lead consumers to make individual choices.
- **Social Media Empowerment:** Platforms give discerning buyers a voice to hold brands accountable, amplify ethical alternatives, and connect with like-minded people.

Implications for Brands

- **Values Can't Be an Afterthought:** Purpose needs to be baked into the core of a business, not just a marketing tactic.
- **Transparency is Key:** Consumers want to know the good, the bad, and how companies are working to improve.
- **Community Matters:** Brands must nurture genuine relationships with customers, fostering trust and loyalty beyond the transaction.
- **Price Isn't Everything:** While competing on value matters, discerning buyers accept some premium for ethical choices.
- **Adaptability is Essential:** Consumer expectations evolve rapidly. Brands can't afford to get complacent.

4. Definition of purpose-driven marketing and why it matters in 2024

Definition of Purpose-Driven Marketing

Purpose-driven marketing is a strategy where a brand's core messaging and campaigns center around a social cause or positive impact that goes beyond simply selling products or services. This purpose aligns with the company's mission and values, creating an authentic connection with consumers who share those values.

Key Elements

- **Authenticity:** The purpose must be deeply rooted in the company's beliefs, not a surface-level tactic.
- **Action:** Purpose-driven marketing involves concrete initiatives supporting the cause, not just words.
- **Long-term Commitment:** This isn't about one-off campaigns, but a consistent theme across brand communications.
- **Storytelling:** Connecting with consumers emotionally through stories that showcase the shared purpose.
- **Consumer Participation:** Inviting customers to be part of the positive impact amplifies the reach.

Why It Matters in 2024

- **The Trust Deficit:** Continued corporate scandals and cynicism fueled by social media make authenticity more valuable than ever. Consumers gravitate toward brands they believe in.
- **Gen Z and Millennial Influence:** These demographics, now a dominant consumer force, are known for prioritizing values-based spending. Brands need to connect with them on this level to succeed.
- **Changing Expectations:** Purpose-driven marketing is increasingly the norm, not the exception. Companies lacking a clear 'why' risk seeming out of touch.
- **Competitive Advantage:** Purpose can build deep brand loyalty, differentiating a company in a crowded market. Done well, it inspires advocacy that traditional marketing can't buy.
- **Attracting Talent:** Purpose-driven organizations are more likely to attract and retain top employees who want their work to have meaning.

Things to Note:

- **Purpose Is Not One-Size-Fits-All:** Effective messaging depends on knowing your audience and finding causes that resonate with them.
- **Avoiding "Woke-washing":** Superficial or bandwagon causes will backfire with discerning buyers.

Case studies of successful purpose-led campaigns

Large Brands:

- **Dove: Real Beauty Campaign:** This long-running campaign challenged narrow beauty standards, featuring diverse women and promoting body positivity. It resonated deeply with consumers tired of unrealistic imagery, contributing to Dove's brand strength and increased sales.
- **Patagonia: Environmental Activism:** Patagonia puts environmentalism at the forefront of everything they do. From their "Don't Buy This Jacket" campaign discouraging overconsumption to donating 1% of sales to environmental causes, their commitment to sustainability has built a fiercely loyal customer base.
- **Nike: Support for Colin Kaepernick:** Nike's decision to feature Colin Kaepernick in their "Dream Crazy" ads, despite controversy around his social justice protests, sparked both backlash and praise. It ultimately strengthened their connection to consumers who identify with the values of speaking out against inequality.

Smaller/Mid-sized Brands:

- **TOMS: The One-for-One Model:** TOMS built their brand on a promise: for every pair of shoes purchased, they'd donate a pair to a child in need. This simple but powerful purpose model resonated with consumers and propelled their growth.
- **Lush Cosmetics: Fighting Animal Testing:** Lush's vocal stance against animal testing, use of ethically sourced, often unpackaged products, and support for various causes has built a following of devoted customers who share their values.
- **Ben & Jerry's: Flavor-Based Activism:** Ben & Jerry's infuses social justice messaging throughout their brand, from naming ice cream flavors to supporting grassroots campaigns. Their willingness to take a stand on issues makes them a favorite among purpose-driven consumers.

Important Notes:

- **Success is Multifaceted:** These campaigns succeeded by combining a strong message, authentic actions, and compelling storytelling, not just by choosing the 'right' cause.
- **Imperfect Is Okay:** Even large brands sometimes face criticism for not going far enough. What's important is demonstrating commitment to improvement.
- **Scalability:** Smaller brands can show purpose in impactful ways, like through local partnerships or transparent sourcing.

6. How to find your authentic brand purpose.

Why Start With "Why"
Before crafting messaging, it's crucial to identify the genuine reason your company exists beyond generating profit. This core purpose informs your actions, shapes your values, and attracts the right customers.

Key Questions to Ask

- **Founding Story Revisted:** Why did you start your business? Was it solving a problem, fulfilling an unmet need, pursuing a passion? Your origin story holds clues to your deeper purpose.
- **What Makes You Unique?** What sets you apart from competitors? Is it your process, your expertise, or the specific gap you fill in the market?
- **Values Check:** What principles guide your business decisions? Do you prioritize sustainability, inclusivity, innovation? Your purpose should align with your deeply held company values.
- **What Change Do You Want to See?** Think beyond your product/service. What impact would you like your company to have on the world, your community, or your industry?
- **Who Do You Serve?** Understanding your ideal customer's passions, struggles, and what they value helps align your purpose with theirs.

Practical Tips

- **Get Team Input:** Don't just make this a top-down exercise. Involve employees at all levels to ensure your purpose reflects the company's collective spirit and gets widespread buy-in.
- **Look for Overlap:** Map out answers to the key questions, seeking common themes or recurring passions. This helps you distill your core purpose.
- **Avoid Generic Language:** Aim for a purpose that is specific to your brand, not a vague statement any company could claim.
- **Don't Be Afraid to Evolve:** Especially for younger brands, your purpose can deepen as your business grows. Be willing to revisit it periodically.

Real-World Examples

- **Warby Parker:** They didn't just sell glasses, they aimed to democratize access to affordable eyewear, tackling a problem faced by millions.
- **The Honest Company:** Founded by Jessica Alba, their commitment to non-toxic baby and home products stemmed from concerns about harmful chemicals most parents share.
- **Local Coffee Roaster:** Their purpose might center on supporting ethical sourcing of beans, building community through their space, or educating consumers about quality coffee.

Remember:
Authenticity is non-negotiable. Customers can spot a mismatch between stated purpose and actions. Make sure your purpose drives your business, not just your marketing.

7. What brand activism looks like in practice.

What Brand Activism IS:

- **Values put into action:** It's about a company taking a public stand on a social or political issue that aligns with their core purpose and actively working to support that cause.
- **Beyond awareness-raising:** Brand activism involves tangible contributions, using a company's resources, platforms, and influence to create change.
- **Aligning with consumer values:** Activist brands resonate with customers who want to see those values reflected in where they spend their money.

What Brand Activism ISN'T:

- **Performative "woke-washing":** Merely changing a logo for Pride Month or issuing a vague statement without follow-up action is not true activism.
- **Profit-driven:** While activism can positively impact sales, it shouldn't be the primary motivation.
- **Universal:** Not every brand needs to engage in activism, and doing so poorly is worse than staying silent.

Forms Brand Activism Can Take:

- **Donations & Partnerships:** Supporting non-profits, grassroots movements, or campaigns financially.
- **Internal Policy Changes:** Altering company practices to be more equitable, inclusive, or sustainable, such as hiring goals or supply chain improvements.
- **Public Advocacy:** Using a brand's platform to amplify messages, lobby for legislative changes, or challenge industry norms related to the issue.
- **Content and Storytelling:** Creating campaigns, documentaries, or social media content that educates and sparks action around a cause.
- **Product Tie-Ins:** Dedicating a percentage of sales to a cause, collaborating with ethical makers, or using product design to raise awareness.

Examples:

- **Ben & Jerry's:** Long-standing commitment to various social justice causes, from flavor names to outspoken CEO statements, and ongoing partnerships.
- **REI's #OptOutside :** By closing on Black Friday and encouraging people to enjoy nature, they tied activism around conservation into their brand identity.
- **Nike's support of Colin Kaepernick:** While controversial, it reinforced their brand values around challenging the status quo and empowering individual voices.
- **Smaller examples:** Local shops donating space for community groups, companies offering employee time for volunteering, etc.

Important Considerations:

- **Authenticity:** The issue MUST align with core brand purpose; otherwise, it'll feel opportunistic.
- **Risk:** Activism can polarize, some brands actively court controversy, others choose less 'hot button' issues.
- **Action > Words:** Consumers demand tangible action to go along with any public statements.

8. Potential benefits of brand activism (increased loyalty, attracting new audiences)

Increased Brand Loyalty:

- Deeper Connection: Customers who share a brand's values feel a stronger emotional bond, transcending just liking the product or service. They feel they are part of something bigger.
- Shared Purpose: Activism positions the brand as a partner in working towards a better world, making consumers feel good about supporting the company.
- Advocacy: Customers who strongly align with a brand's stance are more likely to become brand ambassadors, recommending the company to others within their networks.

Attracting New Audiences:

- Reaching Values-Driven Consumers: Especially for Millennials and Gen Z, aligning with social issues is a major deciding factor in buying decisions.
- Positive Differentiation: Activism can help a brand stand out in a crowded marketplace, especially if they pioneer supporting an underserved cause.
- Media Attention: Activist brands often garner media coverage, increasing brand awareness and potentially reaching new segments.

Additional Potential Benefits:

- Employee Morale and Talent Attraction: People want to work for companies making a positive impact, boosting employee satisfaction and attracting top talent.
- Innovation Trigger: Activism can force a company to rethink its processes, from supply chain to marketing, leading to innovative new solutions.
- Building Community: A shared purpose unites like-minded customers and the brand, fostering a sense of belonging and potential collaborations.

Important Considerations:
- Authenticity is Key: If the brand activism seems inauthentic or opportunistic, it will backfire, leading to accusations of "woke-washing" and lost trust.
- Not Without Risk: Taking a stand can alienate some consumers. Brands need to calculate if the potential gains are worth the potential backlash.
- Long-Term Commitment: Activism is not a one-off campaign. Consumers expect consistency and ongoing effort to support the chosen cause.

9. The risks involved and how to navigate them thoughtfully.

Key Risks:

- **Alienating Customers:** Taking a stand on any issue, especially a controversial one, risks alienating consumers who hold opposing views. This can lead to boycotts and negativity aimed at the brand.
- **Accusations of Hypocrisy:** If a brand's actions contradict their stated values, they will be accused of hypocrisy. This severely damages trust and makes consumers cynical about their motives.
- **Backlash from Internal Stakeholders:** Employees, investors, or partners may disagree with the chosen cause or stance. This can lead to internal conflict and harm the company's reputation.
- **"Woke-washing" Perception:** Consumers are savvy to superficial activism. If actions and resources don't back up the messaging, a brand risks being labeled inauthentic and performative.
- **Distracting from Core Business:** If activism overshadows the product or service, it can confuse consumers about what the company actually does and dilute the brand's focus.

Mitigation Strategies:

- Choose Your Battles Carefully: Not every brand needs to weigh in on every hot-button issue. Focus on causes that deeply align with your core purpose and where you can make a genuine impact.
- Do Your Homework: Before going public, thoroughly research the issue, understand different perspectives, and potential consequences for taking a stand.
- Walk the Walk: Ensure internal policies and actions support the cause. Address any contradictions before publicly advocating to avoid hypocrisy accusations.
- Be Transparent and Consistent: Consumers expect follow-through. Be clear about your actions, communicate progress, and be consistent in supporting the cause long-term.
- Acknowledge the Risks: Internally discuss the potential downsides. Have a plan for addressing negative reactions, and be willing to adapt your approach if necessary.
- Start with Small Actions: If uncertain, support causes through internal changes, partnerships, or donations before making large public statements.

It's important to note:
- No brand can please everyone. Some backlash may be unavoidable, particularly when tackling divisive social issues.
- Silence can be a strategic choice. Brands shouldn't feel pressured into activism, especially if they can't commit to authentic action.

10. The backlash against "woke-washing" and performative allyship

What is "Woke-washing" & Performative Allyship?

- Woke-washing: When a company adopts the superficial aesthetics of social justice or awareness to appear progressive, without meaningful actions or internal change backing it up.
- Performative Allyship: Making public statements of solidarity with marginalized groups or causes, but failing to follow through with contributions, policy changes, or using their platform to amplify marginalized voices.

Why the Backlash?

- Savvy Consumers: People increasingly recognize empty gestures. Social media, in particular, makes it easy to compare a brand's words to its actions.
- Demand for Authenticity: Especially among younger generations, there's an expectation that brands will put their values into practice, not just use them for marketing.
- Trust Erosion: Repeated instances of performative activism by major brands make consumers cynical about any company's motives, making genuine efforts harder to believe.

- Activism as a Trend: Some brands try to capitalize on the social awareness trend without understanding the nuances of the issues or being prepared for the long-term commitment.

The Impact on Brands

- Damaged Reputation: Accusations of being "woke-washed" lead to widespread negative social media attention and calls for boycotts.
- Lost Trust: Consumers feel misled and are less likely to believe future brand messaging, even if the company makes changes later on.
- Alienation of Key Demographics: Younger consumers, who tend to be the most values-driven, are turned off by insincerity.
- Internal Conflict: Employees who care about the cause may become demoralized if they see the company's commitment is superficial.

Examples of Backlash:

- Pepsi's Kendall Jenner Ad: The ad trivialized social justice protests and was seen as deeply tone-deaf and exploitative, leading to widespread mockery and criticism.
- Companies making social justice statements in 2020, but with a history of discriminatory practices or silence on those issues in the past.

11. Strategies for building genuine, trust-based relationships with consumers

Transparency as the Foundation:

- Be Honest About Imperfections: Don't try to hide past mistakes or pretend to be perfect. Acknowledge challenges and outline how you're working to improve.
- Behind-the-Scenes Access: Share insights into your processes, sourcing decisions, or even internal struggles. This humanizes your brand.
- Own Up to Mistakes: If something goes wrong, promptly admit it, apologize sincerely, and outline steps to rectify the situation.

Embrace Two-Way Communication:

- Encourage Feedback and Respond: Actively solicit customer opinions through surveys, social media, or dedicated channels. Show you're listening by addressing concerns and implementing suggestions when possible.
- Facilitate Customer Communities: Foster online forums or spaces where customers can connect with each other and the brand. This builds loyalty and offers valuable insights.
- Go Beyond Automated Responses: In customer service interactions, personalize responses and demonstrate empathy, showing individual concerns matter.

Put Values into Action:

- Walk the Walk: Ensure every aspect of your business aligns with your stated values, from employee treatment to environmental practices.
- Support Causes that Matter: Partner with non-profits or initiatives your target audience cares about. Choose actions over just slogans.
- Be Consistent: Values shouldn't be marketing gimmicks. Your commitment to your purpose should be evident in everything you do, year-round.

Focus on the Human Element:

- Tell Real Stories: Feature user-generated content, spotlight employees, or highlight how your product/service makes a difference in people's lives.
- Celebrate Your Customers: Highlight loyal fans, share their testimonials, and genuinely express appreciation for their support.
- A Little Humor Goes a Long Way: Stiff corporate messaging is off-putting. Show your brand has a personality and can have some fun.

Long-Term Mindset:

- Don't Expect Overnight Results: Building trust takes time and consistent effort. Focus on making the right decisions, not just chasing viral moments.
- Be Willing to Adapt: Consumer expectations evolve. Regularly reassess your strategies, staying attuned to what resonates with your audience.
- Measure the Right Things: Look beyond just sales figures. Track customer sentiment, social engagement, and brand perception over time.

12. Why openness about your processes, values and impact matters

Building Trust:

- Counteracting Cynicism: Consumers are skeptical after scandals and greenwashing. Openness demonstrates you have nothing to hide.
- Behind-the-Scenes Intrigue: Transparency about HOW you do things fosters a deeper connection than just showcasing the final product.
- Addressing Concerns: Proactively sharing information can allay potential consumer objections (e.g., ethical sourcing, pricing breakdowns).

Attracting Conscious Consumers:

- Values Matter: Consumers increasingly want to know what a brand stands for and how their choices align with their own values.
- Informed Decision-Making: Providing detailed information allows consumers to make choices that feel right to them, increasing loyalty.
- Shared Purpose: Openness helps consumers feel like they're part of something bigger when they support your brand.

Standing Out from the Crowd:

- Moving Beyond Buzzwords: Many brands claim to be "sustainable" or "ethical." Transparency allows you to prove it with specifics.
- Storytelling Opportunities: Your processes, values, and impact can all become part of compelling brand narratives.
- Attracting Media & Influencers: Brands with a clear, open approach are more likely to get positive attention in a crowded space.

Long-Term Benefits:

- Employee Morale: Employees feel proud to work for a company that is upfront and accountable.
- Adapting to Change: Openness makes it easier to address challenges or shifts in strategy, as you already have the trust of your audience.
- Future-Proofing: As consumer expectations for transparency continue to rise, brands that adopted this approach early on will be well-positioned.

13. How to leverage radical transparency in your messaging

Understand "Radical" Transparency:

- Beyond traditional reporting: It's not just about disclosing the legally required information, but a proactive embrace of openness.
- Vulnerability included: Being willing to share imperfections, challenges you've faced, and how you're working to improve.
- Audience-centric: It's about providing the information that consumers are actually interested in and find relevant.

Key Areas to Apply Transparency:

- Pricing: Break down costs (Everlane's model), explain any increases, or show how pricing reflects commitments like fair wages.
- Ingredients/Materials: Share full sourcing details, be upfront about any controversial components, and highlight what makes you different.
- Sustainability Impact: Use data and reports (if possible), but also be honest about where you still need to do better.
- Labor Practices: Information about where items are made, working conditions in your factories, and pay scales goes a long way.
- Internal Policies: Sharing diversity statistics, salary ranges (Buffer's approach), or even meeting notes can build trust.

Messaging Strategies:

- Make it Digestible: Don't just dump data. Use infographics, videos, and clear language to make information accessible.
- Tell Stories: Highlight personal impacts - profile farmers you source from, customer testimonials on a product's longevity, etc.
- Ongoing & Multi-Channel: Weave transparency into website sections, product descriptions, social posts, newsletters, etc.
- Invite Participation: Ask customers what else they want to know, how can your reporting be even clearer?

Important Notes:

- Start Where You Are: Even small steps matter. Choose one area to be more transparent about and build from there.
- Consistency is Key: This isn't a one-off campaign, but a philosophy shift.
- Embrace the Journey: Show that being better is an ongoing commitment, not a final destination.

14. Case studies of brands excelling with transparency

Everlane: Radical Transparency in Pricing

- **Concept:** Everlane displays a detailed cost breakdown for each product, including materials, labor, and transportation. This allows customers to see exactly where their money goes and the value proposition behind the price tag.
- **Impact:** Everlane has established itself as a leader in ethical fashion by prioritizing fair wages and sustainable practices. Their transparent pricing builds trust and empowers customers to make informed decisions.

Patagonia: Environmental Impact Transparency

- **Concept:** Patagonia publishes a yearly Footprint Chronicles report detailing the environmental impact of their products, from materials to manufacturing and end-of-life options. They openly acknowledge their shortcomings and their efforts to improve.
- **Impact:** Patagonia has fostered a loyal customer base who appreciate their commitment to environmental responsibility. Their transparency allows them to hold themselves accountable while inspiring others to do better.

Buffer: Open Salaries & Internal Processes

- **Concept:** Buffer, a social media management platform, has a radical transparency policy where they publicly share employee salaries and internal documents, including meeting notes and financial reports.
- **Impact:** Buffer's transparency fosters a culture of trust and attracts top talent who value openness and collaboration. It also allows them to showcase their commitment to fair compensation practices.

The Body Shop: Fighting Against Animal Testing

- **Concept:** The Body Shop has a long-standing commitment to being a cruelty-free brand. They are vocal advocates against animal testing in the beauty industry and actively campaign for change.
- **Impact:** Their transparency in this area resonates with customers who care about animal welfare. The Body Shop has become a leader in ethical beauty practices.

Ben & Jerry's: Social Justice Advocacy

- **Concept:** Ben & Jerry's uses their platform to advocate for social justice causes they believe in. They incorporate their values into their product names, flavor choices, and partnerships with social justice organizations.
- **Impact:** Ben & Jerry's has attracted a loyal customer base who share their progressive values. Their transparency about their social stances allows them to connect with customers on a deeper level.

Key Takeaways:
- These brands demonstrate how transparency can be applied in different ways and across various industries.
- The common thread is a commitment to **open communication, sharing information that matters to customers, and acknowledging areas for improvement**.
- By embracing a culture of radical transparency, these brands have built trust, loyalty, and a strong reputation.

15. Possible evolutions of purpose-driven marketing

Increased Specificity and Measurability:

- Beyond broad values: Consumers will demand that brands define their purpose in more concrete terms, focusing on specific issues or measurable goals.
- Data-backed impact: Simply stating a purpose won't be enough. Brands will need to track and communicate the tangible impact their initiatives are having.
- Collaboration for scale: Brands will increasingly partner with non-profits, NGOs, and even competitors to tackle complex social or environmental problems that no single company can solve alone.

Intersectionality and Inclusivity:

- More nuanced understanding: Purpose-driven marketing will move beyond single-issue advocacy to embrace the interconnectedness of social justice issues.
- Focus on marginalized voices: Brands will need to actively center the experiences and needs of those most impacted by social problems, ensuring their activism is inclusive and benefits those communities.
- Internal AND external: Purpose-driven efforts will need to be reflected in all aspects of the business, from hiring practices to ensuring diverse and equitable representation in their marketing.

Democratization of Activism:

- Empowering consumers: Brands will provide tools and platforms for consumers to take action on causes alongside the company, creating a sense of shared ownership in positive change.
- Small business impact: Purpose-driven marketing won't be solely the domain of large corporations. Local businesses will find creative ways to give back to their communities and support causes.
- Purpose-driven influencers: Influencers with strong values and focus on specific causes will become more sought-after partners for brands, lending authenticity to campaigns.

Hyper-Personalization with Purpose:

- Tailored causes: Data will enable brands to understand customers' individual passions and suggest hyper-relevant causes or ways to contribute aligned with the brand's purpose.
- Shared purpose shopping: Platforms or tools might emerge that connect consumers with brands that match their specific values or concerns.
- Micro-activism: Brands will facilitate small but meaningful actions that fit into consumers' lives, making everyday purchases feel more impactful.

Important Considerations:

- Evolving Expectations: What consumers consider 'purposeful' will continue to change. Brands will need to be adaptable and responsive to these shifts.
- Backlash against Bandwagoning: If brands jump on trends without long-term commitment, consumers will call them out even more swiftly.

16. The ongoing importance of consumer trust as a foundational principle

Consumer trust will remain a foundational principle in the future of marketing, perhaps becoming even more crucial due to these factors:

Heightened Skepticism and Information Overload:

- Declining trust in institutions: From political scandals to the spread of misinformation, consumers are increasingly distrustful of traditional institutions and power structures. Brands will need to work even harder to break through.
- The 'fake news' effect: Consumers are wary of manipulated information and worry about the authenticity of online content, making genuine connection even more important.
- Filter bubbles: Algorithms curate what people see, making them more likely to only get information that reinforces their existing beliefs, emphasizing the need for brands to find ways to demonstrate credibility.

The Power of Individual Choice:

- The empowered consumer: The internet gives consumers unparalleled access to information, reviews, and the ability to compare alternatives. Brands can no longer rely on traditional advertising alone.
- Social Proof as Currency: Recommendations from friends, influencers, and online communities heavily sway purchasing decisions. Trust becomes contagious.

- "Voting with your wallet" amplified: Consumers consciously support (or boycott) brands based on their actions, making a company's reputation directly tied to its bottom line.

The Need for Differentiation:

- A crowded marketplace: It's harder than ever for brands to stand out. Trust becomes a key differentiator when price and features are comparable.
- Consumers seek meaning: People want to feel good about their purchases, trust allows them to support brands that align with their values, contributing to a sense of making a difference.
- Loyalty is earned, not a given: Long-term customer relationships will be built primarily on trust, ensuring people return due to shared values and positive association, not just convenience.

The Future of Trust-Based Marketing:

- Transparency is table stakes: Hiding information is no longer an option. Brands must embrace radical transparency to gain credibility.
- Community over campaigns: Nurturing ongoing relationships with customers through shared values will be essential versus one-off sales pushes.
- Collaboration is key: Building trust may increasingly involve partnerships with respected non-profits or watchdogs that endorse a brand's practices.

YOUR BRAND'S VOICE AND LOOK

1. The Power of a Unified Brand

Themes to Emphasize:

- Trust as Currency: In a world of skepticism, a unified brand builds trust faster. Mention how consistency across touchpoints reinforces the idea that a company delivers on its promises.
- Identity Over Advertising: A strong brand identity makes marketing easier and more efficient. Explain how it's the foundation on which campaigns are built, allowing you to focus on authentic messaging, not constantly reinventing the basics.
- Experience as Branding: The modern consumer interacts with brands in numerous ways. Mention how a unified approach ensures a positive, cohesive experience whether they see an ad, visit your website, or have a customer service issue.
- Competitive Advantage: Many businesses underestimate branding. Underscore how this is a chance to get ahead, especially for smaller brands who can't outspend the competition.
- Brand as Promise: A logo is just a symbol. Explain the deeper idea: your brand is the promise you make to customers, and unity in how you present yourself reinforces that promise.

Angles to Consider:

- Emotional Impact: Don't just focus on the logical. Hint at how a memorable brand makes customers feel – understood, excited, a sense of belonging.
- The Long Game: Briefly address how a focused brand identity compounds over time. Each positive interaction strengthens it further.
- Internal Impact: Hint at the employee benefits. When everyone understands the brand's 'why', it improves team morale and aids in attracting talent that fits your culture.

Additional Tips:

- Voice Matters Here Too: Make your intro match the brand's personality. A serious financial firm will sound different than a playful tech startup.
- "Show" a Bit: If space allows, include 1-2 visuals of a brand doing it well (think: Apple's clean design across everything).
- Set the Stakes: End by implying what's lost if brand identity is scattered: missed opportunities, wasted resources, and customer confusion.

Showcases:

Apple:
Unified by: Seamless integration of minimalist design, intuitive interfaces, and aspirational marketing.
Why it works: Their products, stores, website, even packaging all convey the same sense of clean luxury and ease of use. This reinforces their premium position.

Nike:
Unified by: An energetic spirit, celebration of athleticism, and the iconic "Just Do It" messaging.
Why it works: From bold athlete endorsements to youth sports sponsorships, everything they do communicates their focus on performance and pushing yourself.

Dove:
Unified by: Focus on real beauty, diverse representation, and messages of self-acceptance.
Why it works: Their advertising campaigns, product design (the simple bar of soap), and social good contributions share a consistent theme, strengthening their brand identity.

LEGO:
Unified by: Creativity, playful spirit, and the iconic brick itself.
Why it works: Whether in toy stores, movies, or their theme parks, the emphasis on building and limitless potential connects all their touchpoints.

Glossier:
Unified by: Peer-to-peer tone, minimalist yet playful aesthetic, focus on a natural makeup look.
Why it works: They built a cult following because every aspect, from the pink packaging to the relatable user-generated content, feels targeted at a specific demographic.

2. Crafting Your Core Brand Voice

What is Brand Voice?
Brand voice is the distinct personality and style that your brand projects through all its communications. It's how you would describe your brand if it were a person. Think of it as the following:

- **Word Choice:** The specific vocabulary your brand favors (casual vs. formal, technical vs. conversational, humorous vs. serious, etc.).
- **Sentence Style:** How you structure your sentences (short and punchy vs. long and descriptive).
- **Overall Attitude:** The vibe or feeling your brand's communication conveys (playful, authoritative, reassuring, innovative, etc.).

Brand Voice vs. Brand Tone
It's important to understand the difference between voice and tone:

- **Brand Voice:** This is your underlying personality. It remains largely consistent.
- **Brand Tone:** This is how you adjust your voice to suit different situations, platforms, or audiences. For example, your core voice may be friendly and approachable, but you might adopt a slightly more sincere tone for customer service inquiries.

Why Brand Voice Matters
A strong, well-defined brand voice is crucial for:

- **Recognition:** A consistent voice makes your brand instantly identifiable, even if people don't see your logo.
- **Differentiation:** In a crowded market, a unique voice helps you stand out and cut through the noise.
- **Connection:** People connect with brands that have a human, relatable voice. Authenticity builds trust.

- **Consistency:** A well-defined voice ensures that all your marketing messages, from social media to website copy, feel cohesive and on-brand.
- **Brand Equity:** Over time, a strong brand voice shapes consumer perceptions, values associated with your brand, and can even influence purchase decisions.

Example: The Power of Brand Voice
Think of a brand like Nike. Their brand voice is bold, confident, and motivational. Their tagline, "Just Do It," perfectly encapsulates that attitude. Compare that to the brand voice of Dove, which is nurturing, inclusive, and focuses on real beauty. Both are instantly recognizable, distinct, and project the values of their respective brands.

3. Unearthing Your Brand's DNA: The Key to Finding Your Authentic Voice

Your brand's DNA forms the foundation of your brand voice. Understanding who you are at your core is the essential first step in developing a voice that is both authentic and resonant. Think of your brand DNA as the answers to the following questions:

1. Why Do You Exist?
- **Mission:** What's your brand's ultimate purpose? What problem do you solve for your customers?
- **Vision:** What positive change do you aim to create in the world or in your industry?
- **Values:** What fundamental principles guide your business decisions and actions? (e.g., innovation, sustainability, customer-centricity, etc.)

2. What Makes You Unique?
- **Differentiators:** How do you stand apart from competitors? What are your unique strengths or value propositions?
- **Personality:** If your brand were a person, what traits would they have? Are you friendly and approachable, bold and disruptive, knowledgeable and authoritative, or something else entirely?
- **Brand Promise:** What is the core benefit you consistently deliver to your target audience?

How to Dig Deep
Here are a few exercises to help you extract your brand DNA:
- **The "Five Whys" Exercise:** For your mission, ask "why?" five times in a row, digging deeper into your fundamental reason for existing.
- **Brand Archetypes:** Explore common brand archetypes (e.g., the hero, the caregiver, the explorer) to find one that resonates with your brand's personality.
- **Competitive Analysis:** Identify how you're different from the competition. What gaps do you fill in the marketplace?
- **Customer Feedback:** Surveys, reviews, and social listening can reveal how customers see your brand and the value you bring.

Translating DNA into Voice
Once you have a good understanding of your brand's DNA, start translating it into your communication style:
- **Word Lists:** Generate words that align with your mission, values, and personality (e.g., "empowering", "community-driven", "innovative").
- **Dos and Don'ts:** Create guidelines on what kind of language fits your brand and what doesn't.
- **Examples:** Illustrate your desired voice with sample social posts, product descriptions, or email copy.

A Living Document
Your brand DNA is not set in stone. As your business evolves, it's important to revisit and refine your core elements. This will maintain alignment between your internal understanding of the brand and the voice you express externally.
Remember: A strong brand voice starts with knowing who you are. Unearthing your brand DNA is the key to crafting authentic, impactful communication that connects with your audience.

4. Understanding Your Audience: The Key to Resonant Brand Communication

Your brand voice needs to speak directly to the hearts and minds of your ideal customers. The better you understand them, the more effectively you can tailor your communication in a way that deeply resonates. Here's how to know your audience inside and out:

1. Define Your Ideal Customer
- **Demographics:** Go beyond basics like age and location. Consider:
  - Income level
  - Education
  - Job title/industry
  - Family structure
- **Psychographics:** Dig into their:
  - Interests and hobbies
  - Values and beliefs
  - Pain points and challenges
  - Goals and aspirations

2. Where Do They Hang Out?
- **Online:** Which social media platforms do they favor? What blogs, websites, or online communities do they frequent?
- **Offline:** What events do they attend? Where do they shop? What publications do they read?

3. How Do They Talk?
- **Language and Slang:** Do they use industry jargon, casual language, or specific lingo that identifies them as part of a group?
- **Tone Preferences:** Do they prefer formal, friendly, humorous, or technical communication?
- **Where do they seek information:** Do they rely on peers, expert reviews, or search engines to make decisions?

Gathering Insights
Here are effective ways to collect this valuable audience data:
- **Market Research:** Analyze existing industry reports and studies.
- **Customer Surveys:** Ask direct questions about demographics, interests, and online behavior.
- **Social Listening:** Monitor conversations on social media to see how people talk about your industry and related topics.
- **Website and social analytics:** Examine your existing audience data for patterns and insights.
- **Interviews:** Conduct in-depth interviews with a sample of your target audience for qualitative insights.

Creating Customer Personas
Personas are fictional representations of your ideal customers. They help you visualize and empathize with your audience. Include details like:
- **A Name and Photo:** Make your persona feel like a real person.
- **Demographics and Psychographics:** Summarise their key traits.
- **A Day in the Life:** Outline their typical routines and challenges.
- **Quotes:** Capture their voice and language in imagined quotes.

Using Your Audience Understanding
Refer to your personas and audience research when:
- **Crafting Your Brand Voice:** Ensure your language, tone, and style match the preferences of your audience.
- **Writing Content:** Address their pain points, answer their questions, and speak to their aspirations.
- **Choosing Channels:** Focus marketing efforts where your audience spends their time.

It's Not Static!
Your audience may evolve over time. Regularly revisit your customer personas and research to ensure your communication remains relevant and effective.
Remember: Successful brand communication is a two-way conversation. Understanding your audience allows you to speak in a way that not only gets heard but truly connects.

5. From Traits to Language: Crafting Your Brand's Unique Voice

Once you've defined your brand's DNA and understand your audience, the next step is to turn those abstract concepts into the actual words and phrases your brand will use. This process bridges the gap between brand identity and practical implementation of your voice.

Start with Traits
Review your brand's core personality traits. Are you:
- Friendly & Approachable
- Bold & Innovative
- Luxurious & Sophisticated
- Humorous & Playful
- Authoritative & Knowledgeable

Build Word Lists
For each trait, brainstorm a list of related words and phrases. Consider:
- **Synonyms:** Look up synonyms to find more nuanced ways to express your traits.
- **Connotations:** Be mindful of subtle connotations certain words might carry.
- **Industry Jargon:** Do you want to include industry-specific terms (to sound knowledgeable) or avoid them (to be more accessible)?

Example: "Innovative" Trait
- Word List: cutting-edge, revolutionary, transformative, disruptive, forward-thinking, game-changing

Create Dos & Don'ts
Develop simple guidelines for what to use and what to avoid:
- **Do** use active verbs and strong adjectives to convey energy.
- **Don't** overuse clichés or corporate buzzwords.
- **Do** align vocabulary with your target audience's level of understanding.
- **Don't** use language that feels inauthentic or misleading.

Illustrate with Examples
Transform your word lists and guidelines into real-world examples:
- **Social Media Posts:** How would your brand announce a new product launch with different voice traits (friendly vs. authoritative)?
- **Website Copy:** Write variations of a product description to convey different tones (playful vs. technical).
- **Customer Service Responses:** How would you handle a complaint while maintaining your brand voice?

Consistency is Key
Create a brand voice guide or style sheet that includes:
- Core brand traits
- Word lists
- Dos and Don'ts
- Examples
- Notes on tone variations for different situations

Remember, It's an Ongoing Process
As your brand evolves, and language trends change, revisit your word lists and examples. Regularly audit your content to ensure consistency and that your voice still aligns with your brand identity.
The power of language lies in its ability to convey personality and evoke emotion. By thoughtfully translating your brand's traits, you'll create a voice that truly resonates with your audience and sets you apart.

6. Crafting Your Brand Voice Chart: A Quick-Reference Guide for Consistency
A brand voice chart is an essential tool for ensuring that everyone involved in your brand's communication is on the same page. It translates the intangible concept of brand voice into a clear, easy-to-use reference, helping maintain consistency across all your marketing and communications efforts.

Key Components of a Brand Voice Chart
1. **Core Voice Traits:** List your 3-5 primary brand personality traits (e.g., friendly, innovative, reassuring).
2. **Voice Descriptions:** Briefly describe what each trait means for your brand's communication style in a sentence or two.
    - **Example: Friendly: We are warm, approachable, and use conversational language that makes our customers feel like they're talking to a friend.**
3. **Vocabulary Guide:** Include:
    - Do Use: A list of words and phrases that embody your voice.
    - Don't Use: Words to avoid, as they clash with your desired tone.
4. **Example Sentences:** Demonstrate how your voice comes to life in different scenarios:
    - Social media caption
    - Product description
    - Email newsletter headline
    - Customer service response
5. **Situational Adaptations:**
Briefly outline how your tone might shift in different situations while maintaining your core voice. (Example: A playful social media post vs. a more formal press release.)

Designing Your Chart
- **Keep it Simple:** The goal is a quick reference, not a novel.
- **Visually Appealing:** Use colors and typography that align with your brand.
- **Accessible:** Share digitally and/or have printed copies for your team.

Examples to Inspire You
Search online for "brand voice chart examples" to see various formats and approaches. Some brands even make theirs publicly available!

How to Use Your Voice Chart
- **Onboarding:** Introduce the chart to new team members or external partners.
- **Content Creation:** Refer to it when writing marketing materials, social posts, etc.
- **Training:** Use it as a guide for customer service or sales team training.
- **Audits:** Periodically compare your content to the chart to identify inconsistencies.

A Living Document
Your brand voice may evolve slightly over time. Review and update your chart annually or whenever you make significant brand changes.

Additional Considerations
- **Collaborate:** Involve writers, marketers, and customer service reps in the development of your chart.
- **Advanced Charts:** Larger brands may have separate charts for sub-brands or specific channels.

Remember, consistency is crucial for building a strong brand identity. A well-crafted voice chart ensures your brand always sounds like itself, no matter who is crafting the message.

7. Adapting Your Voice Across Platforms

Adapting Your Voice Across Platforms: Consistency with a Twist
Your brand voice is the foundation of how you communicate, but it shouldn't be completely rigid. Understanding how to flex your tone and style across different platforms is crucial for truly connecting with audiences on their own turf. The key is to remain true to your core personality while tailoring your approach to the unique expectations and nuances of each channel.

Factors to Consider
1. **Audience Demographics:** Does the platform skew younger or older? More professional or casual? Your audience's general makeup on each platform will influence your approach.
2. **Platform Purpose:** Is the platform mainly for:
   - Networking (LinkedIn): More professional tone likely required.
   - Entertainment (TikTok): Playfulness and aligning with trends are key.
   - News & Information (X): A timely and potentially more authoritative voice
   - Building Community (Facebook groups): Conversational and personable
3. **Content Formats:** Consider:
   - Text-heavy vs. visually driven platforms (long blog posts vs. Instagram focus)
   - Live video vs. static posts
   - Opportunities for interaction (encouraging comments and dialogue)

How to Adapt
- **Adjust Formality:** Maintain your core traits but tweak formal vs. casual language on a spectrum, not an on/off switch,
- **Humor:** Is subtle wit appropriate, or should you embrace trending memes? Understand platform expectations.
- **Length:** Adapt long-form, informative content (blog) into quick-hit, attention-grabbing snippets for social.
- **Hashtags & Trends:** Leverage relevant trends and hashtags where appropriate for the platform, ensuring it aligns with your brand.
- **Engagement:** Adapt your tone for interactions, being helpful and empathetic in customer service vs. playful in comments.

Preserve Your Core
While adapting, always ask yourself: "Does this still sound like us?" Remember these essentials:
- **Core Traits:** Your fundamental personality traits shouldn't change drastically.
- **Values Alignment:** Don't sacrifice your brand values for the sake of fitting in on a platform.
- **Visuals Matter:** Ensure images, videos, and design consistently support your voice adaptation.

Voice Chart Expansion
Consider adding a section to your brand voice chart for each major platform you use, outlining:
- Audience specifics on that platform
- Tone adjustments (e.g., slightly more playful on Twitter)
- Examples of ideal content for the platform

It's About Nuance, Not Reinvention
Adapting your voice is about staying true to your brand while understanding the language and social norms of each platform. Don't be afraid to experiment, but always ensure your communications feel authentic.
Remember: Successful brand voice adaptation demonstrates that you understand and value your audience on each platform, building stronger connections in the digital landscape.

Showcases:
- **Mailchimp:**
  - **Core Voice:** Playful, witty, slightly quirky, always helpful.
  - **Adaptations:**
    - **Website:** Longer-form content, educational tone, but retains playful language and visuals.
    - **Twitter:** Embraces short-form humor, trending topics, relevant GIFs, while staying true to brand personality.
    - **Email Newsletters:** Conversational, helpful, friendly, with a dash of their signature wit sprinkled in.
- **Innocent Drinks:**
  - **Core Voice:** Friendly, genuine, focus on sustainability and healthy ingredients.
  - **Adaptations:**
    - **Packaging:** Uses whimsical language, playful design, and direct address to the consumer ("Hello, thirsty person").
    - **Social Media:** Continues the friendly and lighthearted tone, engages with followers, emphasizes community and their mission.
    - **Website:** Includes more educational content on its 'goodness' while maintaining approachable language.
- **Old Spice:**
  - **Core Voice:** Bold, humorous, surreal, over-the-top.
  - **Adaptations:**
    - **Commercials:** Iconic for their outlandish humor and memorable one-liners.
    - **Social Media:** Maintains the playful, unexpected tone in shorter formats, interacts with users in a tongue-in-cheek way.
    - **Website:** While visually aligned, the copy becomes less surreal and more focused on product benefits.

Key Takeaways
- **Strong Core Voice is Key:** Effective adaptation relies on a well-defined brand personality as the foundation.
- **It's About Nuances:** Think about adjusting formality, humor levels, and length, without completely changing who you are.
- **Consistency with Flexibility:** Find the balance between recognizing each platform's rules and injecting your brand's unique personality.

8. Defining Your Visual Identity

Defining Your Visual Identity: The Power of Visual Storytelling
Visual identity is the collection of visual elements that represent your brand and help you create a cohesive, memorable impression. Just as your brand voice communicates your personality, your visual identity does so through design.

Key Components of Visual Identity
- **Logo:** The cornerstone of your visual identity; a unique symbol or mark that represents your brand.
- **Color Palette:** A curated selection of colors that reflects your brand personality and evokes specific emotions (think: calming blue vs. energizing red). Includes primary and secondary colors.
- **Typography:** The fonts you choose for headlines, body text, and other applications. Typography influences both readability and the overall feel of your brand (modern sans-serif vs. classic serif).
- **Imagery:** The kind of photos, illustrations, and graphics you use. This could range from minimalist icons to bold, colorful photography.
- **Layout & Design:** How you arrange visual elements across marketing materials, your website, and other touchpoints. This shapes the overall user experience.

How to Define Your Visual Identity
- **Align with Your Brand Essence:** Your visual identity should support and enhance your brand voice, mission, and values. Refer back to your brand DNA work.
- **Consider Your Audience:** Visual preferences vary. A luxury brand might use sleek visuals, while a brand targeting children might be more playful.
- **Competitive Research:** Analyze your competitors' visual choices to ensure you stand out in a visually compelling way.
- **Seek Inspiration:** Explore design trends, but don't simply copy. Make choices that express your unique brand identity. Pinterest, Dribble, or Behance are great starting points.
- **Create a Style Guide:** Document your choices (logo variations, color codes, fonts, image guidelines, etc.) to ensure consistency across everyone creating assets for your brand.

The Power of Visuals
- **Instant Recognition:** A strong logo and consistent visuals make your brand recognizable even at a glance.
- **Emotional Connection:** Colors, imagery, and design choices can evoke feelings that align with your brand.
- **Differentiation:** In a crowded marketplace, unique visuals help you stand out and avoid looking generic.
- **Trust Building:** Consistent and professional visuals build credibility and trust with your audience.

Remember: Your visual identity is not just about aesthetics; it's a powerful tool for communicating your brand's essence and building a lasting connection with your audience.

Showcases:
- **Apple:**
    - Minimalist aesthetic: Clean lines, ample white space, focus on product photography.
    - Colors: Monochromatic with occasional pops of color.
    - Result: Evokes sophistication, innovation, a premium feel.
- **Target:**
    - Bold & Playful: Emphasis on their signature red, whimsical illustrations, clean layouts.
    - Colors: Red, white, and playful secondary colors.
    - Result: Feels fun, accessible, and conveys a sense of value.
- **Spotify:**
    - Vibrant & Eclectic: Duotone gradients, bold imagery, diverse illustrations.
    - Colors: Iconic green, black, with a variety of accent colors.
    - Result: Expresses creativity, energy, and the breadth of music on the platform.
- **Patagonia:**
    - Nature-Inspired: Stunning outdoor photography, earthy color palettes, rugged textures.
    - Colors: Blues, greens, browns, inspired by nature.
    - Result: Authentic, reinforces their commitment to sustainability and adventure.

How to Analyze Visual Identity
When looking at any brand, consider asking yourself these questions:
- **What emotions does the design evoke?** Is it calm, playful, luxurious, etc.?
- **Color Psychology:** Are the color choices in line with expected industry associations (green for eco-friendly) or do they subvert expectations?
- **Consistency:** Do they use these visuals across website, social media, packaging, etc.?
- **Does it align with their voice?** Does the personality expressed visually match how they sound in their messaging?

9. Ensuring Consistency

Ensuring Consistency: The Key to a Powerful Brand Presence
Consistency means delivering a cohesive brand experience across all customer touchpoints. It's what makes your brand instantly recognizable and builds trust over time, regardless of whether someone sees your logo, reads your emails, or walks into your store. Here's how to achieve that crucial consistency:

1. Establish a Clear Brand Foundation
- **Brand Voice Chart:** Document your core traits, dos and don'ts, vocabulary examples, and tone adaptations for different situations (see previous resources!).
- **Visual Style Guide:** Outline logo usage, color palette, fonts, image styles, and layout principles.

2. Empower Your Team
- **Onboarding & Training:** Make the brand guidelines a key part of training for anyone who creates content or interacts with customers.
- **Accessibility:** Ensure style guides are easily accessible in a central location, whether it's a shared document or an internal brand portal.
- **Collaboration:** Encourage open communication between marketing, sales, customer support, and any external agencies.

3. Tools for Consistency
- **Templates:** Create branded templates for social media posts, email newsletters, presentations, etc.
- **Digital Asset Management (DAM):** Store approved images, logos, fonts in a central hub so everyone uses the latest versions.
- **Content Management System (CMS):** Choose a CMS that allows for easy branding and templated design across your website.
- **Tech for Voice:** Some software offers tone analysis and brand word checks to help writers stay aligned.

4. Audit and Refine
- **Regular Content Audits:** Review your website, social media, and marketing materials. Spot any inconsistencies?
- **Gather Feedback:** Survey customers or use social listening tools to see if your brand presentation feels cohesive from their perspective.
- **Update as Needed:** Don't be afraid to update your guidelines as your brand evolves or if you identify areas for improvement.

Consistency Across Channels
Pay attention to these areas for maximum impact:
- **Visuals:** Using your brand colors, fonts, and imagery everywhere.
- **Messaging:** Align marketing copy, product descriptions, and customer service scripts with your core voice.
- **Brand Values:** Ensure sustainability commitments, company culture, etc., are reflected consistently across touchpoints.

The Rewards of Consistency
- **Stronger Recognition:** The more consistent you are, the faster people will recognize you.
- **Enhanced Trust:** Consistency breeds confidence, assuring consumers they get the same brand experience every time.
- **Differentiation:** Standing out is easier when you're not sending mixed messages.
- **Efficient Operations:** Templates and clear guidelines save time and reduce errors.

Remember: Consistency isn't about being rigid; it's about delivering a reliable experience that aligns with the promises you make as a brand.

10. The Evolution of Your Brand Persona

The Evolution of Your Brand Persona: Adapting to Stay Relevant
Your brand persona, the embodiment of your brand voice and identity, shouldn't be set in stone. As your company grows, the market changes, and consumer preferences shift, it's essential to assess and evolve your persona to ensure it continues to resonate with your audience. Here's how to manage this process:

Why Brand Personas Evolve
- **Company Growth:** Expanding product lines, new target markets, or a broader mission might necessitate tweaking your brand personality.
- **Market Shifts:** Consumer trends, competitor actions, or cultural changes might call for adapting your tone or communication style.
- **Audience Feedback:** Negative feedback, declining engagement, or evolving customer demographics may highlight a need for change.
- **Rebranding:** Significant shifts in your business strategy may require a more extensive brand persona overhaul.

Signs It's Time to Evolve
- **Feels Outdated:** Your brand voice or visuals no longer align with current trends or your company's direction.
- **Doesn't Resonate:** Your messaging doesn't seem to connect deeply with your target audience.
- **Inconsistency Emerges:** Maintaining voice consistency becomes challenging as new people join your team.
- **Competitors Adapt:** If competitors reposition themselves successfully, it might signal a need for you to refine your stance.

The Evolution Process
1. **Revisit Your Foundation:** Review your original brand DNA work. Are your mission, values, and differentiators still accurate?
2. **Analyze Data & Feedback:** Dive into:
    - Customer surveys and reviews
    - Social listening insights
    - Website analytics
    - Sales team observations
3. **Identify Shifts:** What about the market, the audience, or your company requires a change in how you present yourself?
4. **Update, Don't Overhaul:** Focus on subtle adjustments rather than a complete persona change, unless absolutely necessary.
5. **Document Changes:** Update your voice charts and style guides to reflect the evolution, ensuring consistency.
6. **Gradual Rollout:** Introduce changes gradually across content and channels, monitor audience response.

Remember: Evolution is about refinement, not a total personality change. You want to stay true to your core brand DNA while ensuring your communication feels fresh and relevant.

Examples of Successful Evolution
- **Old Spice:** Successfully shifted from an outdated persona to one that resonated with a younger audience through humor and bold campaigns.
- **Dove:** Evolved their focus from solely product benefits towards a broader message of real beauty and inclusivity.

BUILDING TOGETHER: CREATING A COMMUNITY

1. The Rise of the Participatory Consumer

- **The Old Model Crumbles:** Once upon a time, brands were the sole storytellers, broadcasting their messages through carefully crafted campaigns. Consumers were a receptive (or sometimes skeptical) audience. This top-down approach is eroding in the digital age.

- **A Revolution of Influence:** Technology has armed consumers with a megaphone. Social media, review platforms, and the ease of content creation have given ordinary people the ability to impact a brand's reputation and reach. They are no longer passive recipients; they're vocal shapers of the conversation.

- **The Psychology of Participation:** Tap into the core motivations behind this shift:
  - **Authenticity Craving:** People trust peers more than polished ads. They want to feel like they're part of a genuine, like-minded community built around a brand.
  - **Desire for Personalization:** Consumers want products and experiences that reflect their unique preferences. Co-creation allows them to have a hand in shaping what they buy into.
  - **The Empowerment Factor:** The internet and social media have given consumers a sense of agency – if they don't like something, they'll say so. And if they love something, they can champion it for all to see.

- **From Spectators to Co-Creators:** Illustrate this through examples:
  - **The Hashtag Challenge:** Brands invite user-generated content, turning customers into marketers. (Example: Dove's #ShowUs campaign promoting body positivity)
  - **Product Development Feedback:** Companies seeking customer input on new features or flavors directly source ideas from their audience. (Example: Lego Ideas platform)
  - **Customer Reviews as Social Proof:** Potential customers heavily rely on real, unfiltered user reviews, granting consumers immense power to influence purchasing decisions.

- **Smart Brands Get It:** Forward-thinking brands understand this isn't a threat, but an incredible opportunity:
  - **Trust Building:** Co-creation fosters trust, as audiences see their input valued.
  - **Marketing Gold:** Authenticity is the new advertising currency – user-generated content and organic advocacy often outperforms staged campaigns.
  - **A Richer Understanding:** Direct consumer feedback provides invaluable market research and insights.

The Takeaway: The participatory consumer isn't a trend; it's a fundamental shift in how brands and their audiences interact. Embracing collaboration isn't just a marketing tactic anymore; it's essential for building lasting brand loyalty in the digital age.

2. Unlocking the Power of User-Generated Content (UGC)

- **What is UGC?**
    - Provide a broad definition: Any content about a brand created by its consumers, not the brand itself.
    - Common Types:
        - Social media posts (photos, videos, mentions)
        - Reviews and testimonials (on websites or third-party platforms)
        - Blog posts or articles
        - Creative submissions to contests or challenges

- **Why UGC Matters: The Key Benefits**

    - **Authenticity is King:**
    Example: 92% of people trust recommendations from peers over traditional brand messaging
    - **Social Proof in Action:** UGC showcases real people using and enjoying your products/services, which strongly influences purchase decisions.
    - **Resourceful Content Creation:** Leverage a vast library of content made by your enthusiastic audience, saving time and money compared to in-house production.
    - **Strengthened Brand Advocacy:** Highlighting UGC makes customers feel valued, encouraging them to create further content and spread the word organically.

- **How to Encourage UGC**

    - **Contests and Challenges:** Launch a themed challenge with a branded hashtag. Offer incentives (prizes, exclusive access, etc.)
        - Example: GoPro's ongoing awards for stunning user-submitted footage
    - **Clear Prompts and Hashtags:** Provide simple, shareable prompts, and easily discoverable hashtags to guide content creation.
        - Example: Aerie's #AerieREAL campaign encouraging unfiltered body positivity
    - **Showcase and Reward Creators:** Feature the best UGC on your channels, tag creators, and offer perks for standout content (this incentivizes continued creation).

Additional Tips:
- **Set Guidelines:** Have clear expectations for content, keeping it aligned with your brand's image.
- **Obtain Permissions:** Always ask for explicit permission before using anyone's content.
- **Personalize Your Response:** When reposting UGC, don't just reshare – thank creators with genuine interactions to nurture relationships.

Case Study 1: GoPro

- **The Strategy:** GoPro's entire brand ethos is built around user-generated content. They encourage customers to share their most epic, adventurous moments captured with their cameras.

- **Tactics:**
    - "Million Dollar Challenge" offering cash prizes for the best user submissions.
    - Frequent feature of stunning UGC on their website and social channels.
    - Focus on quality – showcasing how their product empowers truly breathtaking visuals.

- **Results:**
    - A massive, self-replenishing library of thrilling, marketing content.
    - Creates a sense of community and excitement around the brand.
    - The footage speaks for itself, showing the power and versatility of their cameras far more effectively than staged ads could.

Case Study 2: Aerie (Sub-brand of American Eagle)

- **The Strategy:** Aerie made a bold move by ditching retouched models for their #AerieREAL campaign. They encourage women to share unedited photos of themselves in Aerie products, celebrating all body types.

- **Tactics:**
    - A simple, empowering branded hashtag.
    - Active reposting of UGC on Aerie's own feeds, giving real women the spotlight.
    - A commitment to never retouching or altering UGC.

- **Results:**
    - Generated huge buzz and positive brand sentiment.
    - Sales increases as women felt represented and inspired.
    - Built a loyal community around body positivity and authentic brand-consumer connection.

3. Influencer Partnerships: More Than Just Promotion

Challenge the Stereotype: Open by dispelling the notion that influencer marketing is simply paying for social media shoutouts. Emphasize that effective partnerships go far beyond transactional product placement.

The Influencer Evolution:

- **Focus on Niche Alignment:** Prioritize influencers whose content and audience naturally align with your brand, even if they have a smaller following. Authenticity and genuine connection matter more than raw follower count.

- **Seek Out Creators, Not Just Promoters:** Look for partners with strong content creation skills who can bring your brand and products to life in exciting, engaging ways.

The Goals Beyond Awareness:

- **Targeted Campaigns:** Highlight how influencers can serve very specific objectives:
    - Driving product trial (exclusive discount codes)
    - Educating about complex offerings
    - Boosting event attendance through influencer promotion
    - Reaching new demographics an influencer taps into

- **Metrics Matter:** Discuss aligning your goals with the right KPIs (not just reach) – affiliate links, content engagement, website traffic, etc.

- **Co-Creative Collaborations:** This is where influencer campaigns truly shine.

- **Limited Edition Products:** Partner with an influencer to develop a product/line – their audience insights ensure market fit.

- **Content Series:** Have them create educational or entertaining content featuring your offerings.

- **Giveaways and Experiences:** Influencer-led contests and unique brand experiences build hype and lasting connection.

The Value of Diverse Voices:

- **Representation is Key:** Consumers want to see themselves reflected in brand campaigns. Work with creators across races, body types, abilities, and lifestyles.

- **Niche Communities:** Micro-influencers often boast highly engaged, passionate audiences – tap into these specific interests.

Strong examples of successful influencer co-creations:

- **Becca Cosmetics x Chrissy Teigen:** This partnership resulted in a wildly popular makeup collection featuring Teigen's signature "glowy" look. Her involvement extended beyond just being the face of the campaign – she helped select shades, packaging, and product names. This collaboration sold exceptionally well and boosted brand visibility for Becca Cosmetics.

- **ColourPop Cosmetics x Becky G:** The singer Becky G co-created multiple makeup lines with ColourPop, incorporating elements reflecting her Latinx heritage and vibrant personality. These collections often sell out quickly, demonstrating the power of an influencer who genuinely infuses the product line with their own style and connects directly with their fan base.

- **Quay Australia x Desi Perkins:** The popular eyewear brand Quay has an ongoing partnership with beauty influencer Desi Perkins. They've collaborated on multiple sunglasses collections that consistently become best-sellers. Perkins' input on design and style taps directly into what her loyal following loves.

- **Outdoor Voices:** This activewear brand actively collaborates with fitness instructors, yoga teachers, and wellness-focused micro-influencers. By tapping into these niche communities, they create authentic content that highlights the practicality and style of their apparel in real-life scenarios.

- **Tarte Cosmetics:** While now a larger brand, Tarte Cosmetics built its initial popularity by partnering with beauty bloggers and smaller makeup influencers. Sending out products for review and creating affiliate programs helped them gain visibility and credibility within the beauty-enthusiast community.

- **M.Gemi:** This handcrafted Italian shoe brand leveraged style influencers within specific niches (petite fashion, sustainable fashion, etc.). These partnerships highlighted the quality of their shoes in a targeted way, reaching audiences interested in their specific values.

4. The Ethics of Collaboration

Introduction: The Responsibility of Power: As brands embrace collaboration, acknowledge that they often hold a greater position of power within these partnerships. With this comes the responsibility to act ethically.

Transparency: The Foundation of Trust

- **Disclosure is Key:** Clearly identify any paid partnerships, whether with major influencers or when compensating for UGC. Consumers deserve to know when content is sponsored.
- **Respecting Copyright:** Always obtain proper permissions before using user-generated content. Offer credit and consider additional compensation when appropriate.

Fair Compensation: Beyond Exposure

- **The "Exposure" Trap:** While exposure has some value, it doesn't pay bills. Smaller influencers and content creators deserve fair payment for their time and creative work.
- **Negotiating Power:** Help readers understand guidelines for fair compensation models (flat fee, affiliate links, revenue share, etc.) and how to negotiate contracts that benefit all parties.
- **Valuing Everyone's Contribution:** Even when collecting UGC without direct payment, consider alternative forms of recognition (gift cards, product, exclusive benefits) as a way to show appreciation.

Embracing Diversity

- **Representation Matters:** Make a conscious effort to work with creators from diverse backgrounds, amplifying underrepresented voices in your industry.
- **Intersectionality:** Consider race, gender, sexual orientation, disability status, and other factors when aiming to reflect your full audience.
- **Avoid Tokenism:** Collaborations should be genuine and meaningful, not just checking a diversity box.

Negative Examples:

Example 1: The "Unpaid Influencer" Fiasco

- Many instances exist, but one common case involves brands, often smaller businesses, reaching out to influencers with offers of "exposure" in exchange for free products or services.
- Backlash occurs when:
  - The influencer has a significant following that warrants fair compensation.
  - The request is unreasonable (large amount of content for mere product).
  - The influencer publicly calls out the brand for the exploitative offer.

Example 2: Racial Pay Disparity

- Several brands have been criticized for offering vastly different compensation to Black and non-Black influencers for similar campaigns.
- This reflects a deeper issue of systemic undervaluing of Black creators' work and reach.
- Brands involved in these scandals often face:
  - Public call-outs across social media.
  - Decreased consumer trust, especially among minority consumers.
  - Difficulty attracting diverse talent for future collaborations.

Example 3: The "Fake Transparency" Scandal

- Some brands attempt to skirt FTC disclosure guidelines around paid partnerships by using vague language or intentionally hiding the fact that content is sponsored.
- When caught:
  - Regulatory bodies might get involved (fines, etc.).
  - Consumers feel deceived, eroding trust in the brand.
  - The influencer involved may also face negative consequences.

Positive Examples:

Example 1: Fenty Beauty

- Rihanna's beauty brand is widely praised for its dedication to inclusivity and representation across all its marketing efforts.
- From the start, their influencer partnerships have prioritized working with a vast range of creators from diverse backgrounds, reflecting their shade range and brand ethos.
- They are known for:
    - Fair compensation practices, even for smaller influencers.
    - Building long-term, genuine relationships with diverse creators.
    - Giving influencers creative input and a voice within campaigns.

Example 2: Dove (Select Campaigns)

- While Dove has had some controversies in the past, certain campaigns stand out as positive examples of ethical collaboration.
- Their #ShowUs Project:
    - Partnered with female photographers worldwide to create a more realistic image library of women.
    - Compensated those photographers fairly for their work.
    - Focused on celebrating body diversity and challenging harmful beauty standards.

Making Stories that Stick

1. The Power of Brand Storytelling

Human Connection is Key: People don't connect with products, they connect with stories. Brand storytelling is about forging those emotional bonds.

Why It Matters:
- **Sticky Marketing:** Stories are inherently memorable. They stick in the mind long after facts and figures fade.
- **Loyalty Beyond Logic:** Customers who feel an emotional connection with your brand are less likely to switch for a cheaper competitor.
- **Stand Out or Fade Out:** In a crowded marketplace, your unique story is what makes you unforgettable.

It's Not Just Ads: Brand storytelling weaves your values and mission into everything you do, shaping how the world perceives you.

Transition: Ready to turn your brand into a captivating story? Let's explore how to find your unique narrative and bring it to life.

2. Human-Centric Stories

The Spotlight Shift: Underline the move from your brand being the hero to your customer becoming the central focus of your stories.

Understanding Your Audience's Journey:
- Pain Points: What problems do they struggle with that your product/service helps solve?
- Aspirations: What are their desires, dreams, or goals?
- Moments of Interaction: Map out the touchpoints where customers encounter your brand (website, social media, in-store, etc.)

Types of Human-Centric Stories:
- Transformation: Showcase how a customer's life improved after using your product/service. (Before and after is classic)
- Community: Highlight the sense of belonging your brand fosters among like-minded individuals.
- Overcoming Obstacles: Share narratives of customers achieving a goal with the help of your brand (tools, support, etc.).
- Shared Values: Feature stories aligning with your brand's mission and your customers' own ideals.

Finding Your Storytellers:
- User-Generated Content: Customer testimonials, reviews, and social media posts are a treasure trove.

- In-Depth Case Studies: Interviewing loyal customers for longer-form success stories.
- "A Day in the Life" Style: Showcasing how your brand seamlessly fits into people's real experiences.

Case Study 1: Dove – The "Real Beauty" Campaign
- Focus: Challenging unrealistic beauty standards and celebrating the diversity of women.
- Human-Centric Approach:
    - Featured real women of all shapes, sizes, and ages in relatable scenarios.
    - Campaigns like "Show Us" used user-generated content to widen representation.
    - Directly addressed the insecurity and self-doubt common in their audience.
- Impact:
    - Campaigns went viral, sparking broader conversations about body image.
    - Strengthened Dove's brand image as inclusive and empowering.
    - Deep emotional connection led to increased customer loyalty.

Case Study 2: Airbnb – "Belong Anywhere"
- Focus: Shifting the focus from just accommodations to the human connections travel fosters.
- Human-Centric Approach:
    - Host testimonials: Emphasizing the personal touch of Airbnb vs. hotels.
    - Traveler stories: Highlighting diverse people finding community and adventure globally.
    - Emphasizes values of acceptance, openness, and creating meaningful experiences.
- Impact:
    - Appeals to a desire for connection beyond the basic tourist experience.
    - Positions the brand as a facilitator of authentic cultural exchange.
    - Fosters a loyal community based on shared traveler values.

Why These Examples Work:

- Audience-Focused: They address core emotions and motivations their target market identifies with.
- Authentic Voices: Leveraging real customer testimonials or user-generated content is powerful.
- Shared Values: The stories tap into broader themes their audiences care about (body positivity, the desire to belong).

3. Emotional Resonance

Defining Emotion's Role: Explain that emotional resonance is what turns a good story into an unforgettable one that shapes how people feel about your brand.

Key Emotional Levers
- Inspiration: Stories of achieving a dream, overcoming obstacles, or acts of kindness.
- Humor: Make your audience laugh or feel a sense of relatable lightness.
- Empathy: Tap into feelings of shared experience and understanding of challenges.
- Surprise: An unexpected twist or element of wonder creates a memorable impact.
- Purpose: Align with your customers' values (sustainability, social justice, etc.)

Storytelling Archetypes:
- Introduce the concept of classic narrative structures that resonate deeply with humans.
- Common Examples:
- Overcoming the Monster: Hero facing a challenge.
- Rags to Riches: Transformation and underdogs triumphing.
- The Quest: A journey with a significant goal.

- How to Adapt: Subtly use these structures while adding your brand's unique spin.

Visual Storytelling:
- Imagery is powerful: The right visuals amplify the emotional effect of your story.
- Consider: Color psychology, symbolism, and authentic, relatable imagery.

Case Study 1: Nike – "Dream Crazy"
- Focus: Celebrating athletes who defied expectations, embracing themes of perseverance and ambition.
- Emotional Levers:
    - Inspiration: Showcases both superstar and everyday athletes overcoming adversity.
    - Empowerment: The "crazy" label is reframed as a badge of honor for those who dare to strive.
    - Shared Values: Positions Nike as a champion of those who push boundaries.
- Impact:
    - Highly viral. Sparked conversations around achieving dreams regardless of obstacles.
    - Strengthened Nike's brand image as motivating and aspirational despite some controversy.

Case Study 2: Always – "Like A Girl"
- Focus: Challenging the negative connotations of the phrase "like a girl" and empowering young women.
- Emotional Levers:
    - Empathy: Highlights the drop in confidence many girls experience during adolescence.
    - Social Purpose: Aligns the brand with a greater cause of gender equality.
    - Inspiration: Reframes "like a girl" as a symbol of strength and limitless potential.
- Impact:
    - Provoked important conversations about societal sexism.
    - Boosted brand perception as a champion for young women.
    - Demonstrated that tackling sensitive topics with authenticity can resonate deeply.

Case Study 3: Apple – Holiday Campaigns
- Focus: Often center around heartwarming stories of connection, family, and the role Apple products play in facilitating those moments.
- Emotional Levers:
    - Nostalgia: Evokes fond memories of the holiday season and childhood wonder.
    - Warmth and Belonging: Depictions of loved ones coming together.
    - Subtle Product Placement: Associates those positive emotions with their devices.
- Impact:
    - Highly anticipated annual tradition.
    - Strengthens Apple's emotional connection with customers, emphasizing the brand's role beyond mere technology.

Important Notes
- **Sincerity is Key:** Audiences can spot forced sentimentality. Find genuine emotional themes that align with your brand.
- **Don't Overdo It:** Subtlety is often more powerful than being overly manipulative with emotions.

4. Omnichannel Storytelling

The Multi-Platform Landscape: Acknowledge that today's audiences interact with brands across numerous channels (website, social media, in-store, etc.).

Consistency is Key, Copying Isn't:
- Core Message: Your brand's overarching story and values should remain the same.
- Adaptations: Tailor the tone, format, and depth to each platform's strengths.

Mapping Your Customer's Journey:
- Where Do They Hang Out? Meet your audience on the platforms they already use
- Different Stages: Consider how your stories serve varying needs throughout the purchase funnel (awareness, deeper interest, conversion).

Omnichannel Techniques:
- Serialized Storytelling: Unfold a longer narrative across multiple touchpoints.
- "Snackable" Content: Create short, impactful stories designed specifically for platforms like Instagram or TikTok.
- User-Generated Content: Encourage customers to share their own experiences as part of your broader brand story.
- Behind-the-Scenes: Give glimpses into your brand's process on visually-oriented platforms.
- Interactive Elements: Quizzes, polls, and choose-your-own-adventure style content get audiences directly involved on specific platforms.

The Power of Visual Storytelling:
- Infographics: Complex info in easily digestible format
- Original Photography: Show your brand's unique personality with visuals tailored to each platform.
- Video's Versatility: Short-form teasers to longer, in-depth narratives depending on the platform.

Key Takeaways
- **Think Like a Content Ecosystem:** How can different pieces of content complement and reference one another?
- **Prioritize Engagement:** Encourage interaction and make audiences feel like participants in the ongoing story.
- **Analyze and Adapt:** Track what kinds of stories resonate on each platform, and tailor your strategy accordingly.

Case Study 1: LEGO
- Omnichannel Approach: Their narrative world seamlessly spans physical products, movies, video games, social media, and in-person experiences.
- Core Themes: Creativity, imagination, and the joy of building are consistent across all platforms.
- Adaptations:
    - Social Media: Focus on user-generated content, showcasing amazing fan builds, and fun, short-form videos.
    - Movies & Games: Expand their story world with new characters and adventures, while retaining a playful spirit.
    - Theme Parks: Bring the LEGO experience to life for immersive, interactive storytelling.

Case Study 2: GoPro
- Omnichannel Approach: Built on user-generated content, featuring breathtaking footage across their platforms.
- Core Message: Empowerment, capturing your own adventures, pushing personal boundaries.
- Adaptations:
    - Website: Longer-form customer stories showcase both product capabilities and inspire action.
    - Social Media: Highlight stunning visuals as quick "wow" moments. Contests and challenges further involve the audience.
    - Brand Events: Sponsor events and athletes aligned with their adventurous brand image.

Case Study 3: REI
- Omnichannel Approach: Content strategy promotes a love for the outdoors and responsible recreation across platforms, alongside product focus.
- Core Message: Expertise, sustainability, and facilitating a connection to nature.
- Adaptations:
  - Blog/Website: In-depth articles on outdoor skills, trip planning, and conservation topics.
  - Social Media: Beautiful photography mixes with inspiring quotes and practical tips.
  - In-Store: Events, classes, and knowledgeable staff reinforcing their brand values in person.

Why These Work:
- Strong Central Narrative: Each brand has a clear core theme that they adapt cleverly.
- Customer as Content Creator: Involving the user makes the story feel shared and authentic.
- Platform Savvy: They understand the strengths and audiences of each channel they use.

5. Beyond Marketing: Internal Storytelling

The Importance of Internal Alignment: Explain that a strong brand story isn't just for external audiences; it's essential for guiding your entire organization.

Values and Mission in Action:
- Define your Why: Craft a clear narrative about your brand's purpose beyond just profits.
- Decision Making: Your story becomes a touchstone for company choices, ensuring they align with your core values.
- Crisis Management: A pre-established value-centric narrative helps navigate difficult situations.

Attracting the Right Talent:
- Employer Branding: Communicate what kind of company culture you're building through your story.
- Shared Purpose: Potential hires who resonate with your mission are more likely to be a good fit long-term.

Employee Engagement and Morale:
- Feeling Part of Something: Stories cultivate a sense of belonging and shared goals.
- Recognizing Success: Highlight employee achievements that directly tie into the broader brand story.
- Brand Ambassadors: Employees who believe in the story will naturally champion the company externally.

Techniques for Internal Storytelling:
- Company Intranet: A hub for sharing ongoing narratives, values, and employee spotlights.
- Regular All-Hands: Leaders reinforce the company story and connect it to current projects.
- Internal Campaigns: Celebrate milestones or initiatives through storytelling techniques.

Key Takeaways
- **Storytelling is Leadership:** Company leaders play a vital role in shaping and embodying the internal narrative.
- **Consistency Matters:** The way you treat employees should mirror the values you project to customers.
- **Long-Term Impact:** A strong internal brand story fosters loyalty, attracts the right people, and aids in weathering challenges.

Case Study 1: Patagonia
- Strong Mission Focus: Their commitment to environmentalism and sustainability deeply shapes both external marketing and internal culture.
- Internal Storytelling:

- - "Footprint Chronicles" on their website details the environmental impact of their products and initiatives, increasing employee awareness.
  - Activism: Encourage employees to engage in causes important to the brand.
  - Values-Driven Growth: Store openings and business decisions are made with their mission in mind, not just profit.
- Impact: Attracts dedicated talent aligned with their ethos, high employee retention, positive brand image externally.

Case Study 2: Zappos
- Strong Focus on Customer Service: Famously empowers employees to go above-and-beyond, reinforcing a customer-centric story.
- Internal Storytelling:
  - Culture Book: Employees annually contribute stories about company values in action.
  - Celebration: Highlighting acts of exceptional customer service reinforces the core narrative.
  - Hiring for Fit: Their interview process prioritizes finding people who embody Zappos' focus on building relationships.
- Impact: Known for excellent service, loyal customer base, fosters a sense of purpose in employees.

Case Study 3: Southwest Airlines
- Fun and Friendly Spirit: Their "fun-loving" external brand image is strongly mirrored in their company culture.
- Internal Storytelling:
  - Employee Recognition: Celebrating quirky achievements and a sense of humor.
  - Leadership Emphasis: CEO is known for being involved and emphasizing a "people first" philosophy.
  - Shared Experiences: Company events and traditions aim to foster a close-knit community feel.
- Impact: Lower turnover rates than industry averages, known for approachable brand image, projects an air of enjoying their work.

6. Storytelling as an Ongoing Journey

The Value of Iteration: Remind readers that exceptional brand stories aren't static; they evolve as your company and audience do.

Key Questions to Revisit:

- Customer Feedback: What resonates with your audience? What do they want more of? Analyze comments, reviews, and social media engagement.
- Your "Why": Does your current story still authentically reflect your company's mission? Are some aspects outdated?
- New Opportunities: Are there emerging trends or platforms to tap into with fresh storytelling angles?

Tools for Staying Agile:

- Social Listening: Monitor conversations about your brand and your industry for insights.
- Regular Audits: Review your current content to see if any themes have become stale or if you're overlooking powerful narratives.
- Embrace Experimentation: Don't be afraid to try new formats or campaigns on a smaller scale to test what connects.

The Rewards of Evolving Your Story:

- Staying Relevant: Avoid stagnation by adapting your story to cultural shifts and new audience needs.
- Deeper Resonance: By constantly honing your story, you'll uncover the most impactful ways to connect with your customers.
- Brand Longevity: Companies that can evolve their story alongside the times remain engaging for the long haul.

Call to Action

- Encourage readers to view their story as a living, breathing entity.
- Provide a question or exercise they can do to immediately audit their current brand storytelling.
- End on a note of possibility, highlighting the exciting journey of continually discovering new ways to connect with their audience.

"The best brand stories aren't just written once; they're an exciting adventure you embark on with your customers, chapter by chapter."

Video Dominance: Formats and Strategies

1. Short-Form Video Explosion

Defining Short-Form: Videos generally under 60 seconds, often closer to 15-30 seconds. This format has seen a meteoric rise in popularity.

The Impact of TikTok:
- Normalize Short Attention Spans: TikTok trained users to consume and create content in easily digestible chunks.
- Trend-Driven Culture: Meme formats, catchy songs, and challenges spread virally, boosting views of user content and brand videos embracing these trends.
- Algorithm is King: The platform prioritizes engagement over large follower counts, giving anyone a shot at virality.

Key Platforms for Short-Form Success

TikTok: The originator. Focus on raw creativity, humor, and following trends.
Instagram & Facebook Reels: Short video format integrated into existing platforms. Leverages your established audience, but content needs to compete in main feeds.
YouTube Shorts: Newer competitor. Good if you already have a YouTube audience, but still finding its footing in terms of algorithm and user habits.

Best Practices for Short-Form:

The First 3 Seconds are EVERYTHING: Grab attention immediately with a surprising visual, relevant question, or trending effect.
Embrace the Trends: Don't be afraid to leverage popular audio, challenges, or humor styles – it increases discoverability.
Utilize Text Overlays: Many people watch with sound off. Captions and text emphasize key points
Optimize for Vertical: The smartphone-dominant format of short-form video.
Call To Action: Even a small "Like for Part 2" or "Follow for more" boosts engagement, which benefits your visibility in the algorithm.

Here are a few real-life examples of brands and creators successfully leveraging short-form video:

Case Study 1: Duolingo
- Platform: Primarily TikTok
- Strategy: The language learning app uses humor, relatable memes, and a quirky mascot to make language learning seem approachable and fun.
- Success:
- Massive following with high engagement on videos.
- Brand personality: Their playful content stands apart from traditional educational marketing.
- Boosted brand awareness among younger demographics.

Case Study 2: Ryan Trahan
- Platform: YouTube Shorts, also active on TikTok and Instagram Reels
- Strategy: Documents his journey to deliver a penny to MrBeast, creating a serialized short-form narrative with daily updates.
- Success:
- Each short video acts as a "cliffhanger," incentivizing followers to stay tuned.
- Achieved rapid growth through consistent, engaging, short videos.
- Built a highly engaged community invested in his journey.

Case Study 3: Chipotle
- Platform: TikTok
- Strategy: Embraces trends with a twist, often showcasing their menu items in funny, relatable scenarios. They partner with influencers and leverage user-generated content challenges.
- Success:
- "#ChipotleLidFlip" challenge went viral, integrating their brand into a trend.
- Feel like they're 'part' of TikTok culture, not just advertising on it.
- Increased positive brand sentiment, particularly among Gen Z and millennials.

Why These Work
- Entertaining First: Their content isn't focused on pushing sales, they offer value through humor or interesting stories.
- Embrace Platform Trends: They utilize platform-specific editing, meme formats, and audio to make their videos feel native.
- Authenticity Matters: Even brands like Chipotle manage to come across as relatable and playful, aligning with the raw nature of short-form video.

2. Long-Form Still Reigns

Countering the "Short Attention Span" Myth: While short-form is dominant, long-form thrives when it offers depth and clear value to the viewer.

Where Does Long-Form Shine?
- Tutorials & How-Tos: Complex processes or detailed instructions
- In-Depth Product Reviews: Provides nuanced information for serious shoppers.
- Storytelling: Documentaries, mini-series, or immersive brand stories that need time to unfold.
- Thought Leadership: Interviews, panel discussions, and webinars
- Live Video: Q&As, behind-the-scenes, or real-time events gain a sense of immediacy and interaction.

Key Platforms:
- **YouTube:** The undisputed king of long-form. Well-developed search, categories, and subscription features for discoverability.
- **Facebook and Instagram:** While short-form dominates feeds, both IGTV and longer Facebook videos exist for dedicated viewers.
- **Live Streaming:** Twitch gaining popularity beyond gaming. Facebook Live still widely used. Tools like Restream allow broadcasting to multiple platforms at once.
- **Niche Platforms:** Vimeo is popular with some creators, and newer options (like Nebula) provide ad-free experiences for niche audiences.

Long-Form Optimization:
- **Strong Titles & Thumbnails:** Catch the eye while scrolling. Tools like TubeBuddy or VidIQ can help analyze competitor titles and keywords.
- **Intros Matter:** Briefly set the stage for what the viewer will gain and why they should keep watching.

- **Pacing & Structure:** A clear outline keeps your content flowing. Chapter markers on YouTube help with navigation.
- **Calls to Action:** Don't just end abruptly – ask viewers to like, comment, subscribe, or visit a site for more.

Key Takeaways
- **Quality Over Quantity:** One well-made long-form video is better than multiple mediocre ones.
- **Cater to Intent:** People seeking long-form content have a specific goal in mind. Help them achieve it efficiently.
- **Repurposing Potential:** Can longer videos be broken into shorter teasers for social media to drive traffic?

Case Study 1: MrBeast
- Platform: YouTube
- Strategy: Known for elaborate, high-budget videos, often stunt-driven or featuring massive challenges.
- Success:
- Production Value: Spectators tune in knowing they'll see visually engaging, unique content.
- Serialization: Multi-part challenges create anticipation and encourage binge-watching.
- Audience Involvement: Occasionally features fans in videos, driving engagement.

Case Study 2: Bon Appétit
- Platform: YouTube
- Strategy: Varied long-form content, focusing on their diverse personalities and culinary expertise. Includes:
- Gourmet Makes: Chefs attempting to elevate junk food.
- Test Kitchen Tours: In-depth look at specific ingredients or techniques
- "Back-to-Back Chef": Celebrities cooking alongside pros with humorous results.
- Success:
- Multiple Series: Caters to different levels of viewer interest.
- Personality Driven: Viewers become invested in the chefs, fostering loyalty.

Case Study 3: Nerdwriter1
- Platform: YouTube
- Strategy: Video essays analyzing art, pop culture, and social issues through a unique lens.
- Success:
- Niche Appeal: Combines intellectual depth with visually creative presentations.
- Passion is Clear: Creator's genuine enthusiasm makes complex topics accessible.
- Thought-Provoking: Encourages discussion and a loyal community in comments.

Why These Examples Work
- **High Value:** They offer something you can't easily get in short-form – spectacle, deep dives, or a sense of shared experience with creators.
- **Cater to Intent:** Viewers are consciously choosing to invest time, so the content rewards that investment.
- **Discoverability:** YouTube's recommendations and search function help these videos find their target audience.

3. Platform-Specific Strategies

The Importance of Nuance: While core storytelling principles remain, each platform has its own algorithms, trends, and best practices to understand.

Key Platforms to Analyze:
- TikTok: Focus on vertical video, trend-hopping, captions, short length for maximum potential reach.
- Instagram Reels: Similar to TikTok, but can integrate with your established feed and Stories for cross-promotion.
- YouTube: Horizontal format. Prioritizes titles, SEO, longer-form content for in-depth discovery.

- Facebook (Video & Live): Wider audience demographics than above platforms. Good for live events, repurposed content, and targeting specific interest groups via ads.

Factors to Consider
- **The Algorithm:** How does each platform prioritize content? What gets shown to users? Research and adjust your approach accordingly.
- **Audience Demographics:** TikTok skews younger, while Facebook has a broader age range. This influences your content style and tone.
- **Features & Formats:** Does the platform support live video, Stories, duets, remixing, etc.? Use native tools to your advantage.
- **Discoverability:** How do people find videos on each platform (hashtags, search, For You page)? Optimize accordingly.

Adaptation, Not Replication
- The Core Story: Remains consistent through a multi-platform approach.
- The Format: Adjusts pacing, visuals, and length based on platform norms.
- Example: A behind-the-scenes product demo could be:
- TikTok: Multiple short clips using trending audio, focusing on the most interesting moments.
- YouTube: A longer, continuous look with more explanation and personality.
- Live (Insta/Facebook): Real-time demo with Q&A, creating a sense of urgency.

Key Takeaways

Do Your Homework: Research current best practices on each platform you intend to use. These things evolve rapidly!

Data is Your Friend: Analyze performance to see what kind of videos do well on each platform, and tailor your content accordingly.

Don't Spread Too Thin: It's better to master a few platforms than do a mediocre job on many.

Case Study 1: The Washington Post
- **Focus:** Their use of TikTok to reach younger audiences with news content.
- **Strategy:**
    - **TikTok:** Short, snappy videos with humorous text overlays summarizing news stories, often leveraging trends and memes.
    - **Instagram:** Similar visual style, but may include links for deeper dives, integration with Stories.
    - **Main Website/Platforms:** Traditional in-depth journalism and longer video pieces.
- **Impact:**
    - **Expanded Audience:** Increased awareness of their brand among younger demographics who don't traditionally consume news.
    - **Maintains Authority:** Their core reporting remains serious, catering to their existing readership.

Case Study 2: Tasty
- **Focus:** Recipe and food-related video content.
- **Strategy:**
    - **Facebook/Instagram:** Originally known for overhead, short recipe videos, often with minimal instruction.
    - **YouTube:** Longer, more detailed recipes, sometimes featuring personalities or collaborations.
    - **TikTok:** Embraces trends, ultra-short versions of recipes, and visually satisfying content (cheese pulls, etc.).
    - **Dedicated Website:** Houses all recipes in a searchable format for those seeking specifics.
- **Impact:**
    - **Platform Mastery:** They understand the strengths and audiences of each platform, catering content accordingly.
    - **Massive Reach:** One of the most successful food media brands across multiple channels.

Why These Examples Work
- Distinct but Connected: Content on each platform feels like it's part of the same brand "world."
- Play to Strengths: They use each platform how it's intended (quick hits on TikTok, deep dives on YouTube).
- Audience Driven: They understand what kind of content their target audience wants on each specific platform.

4. Video Beyond Promotion

The Power of "Show, Don't Tell": Video allows you to demonstrate and humanize even uses that might seem less exciting on paper.

Customer Service Excellence
- **Explainer Videos:** Clear, visual guides for common setup issues, troubleshooting, or product features.
- **FAQs Answered:** Short, focused videos addressing frequent customer questions.
- **Testimonials:** Video testimonials feel more authentic and help build social proof for potential customers.

Internal Use: Video's Value Behind the Scenes
- **Training & Onboarding:** Consistent video modules ensure every new hire gets the same quality information.
- **Culture Building:** Share team successes, highlight outstanding work, or give glimpses into daily company life.
- **Leadership & Communication:** Video messages from executives can boost morale and convey important updates.

Video as Storytelling
- **The Origin Story:** Documentaries or shorter videos about your brand's founding and mission.
- **Employee Spotlights:** Increases customer connection with the individuals behind the business.
- **"A Day in the Life":** Showcases authentic work processes, especially for product-based brands.

Key Takeaways
- **Think Holistically:** Where are there pain points or information gaps that video could solve in your organization?
- **Potential Cost Savings:** Well-made explainer videos can reduce time spent on repetitive customer service or training tasks.
- **Video Strengthens Connection:** Whether it's with customers or internally, video humanizes your brand and builds deeper relationships.

Case Study 1: Wistia
- **Focus:** Wistia themselves are a video hosting and marketing platform. They practice what they preach!
- **Internal Use:** They heavily utilize video for asynchronous team communication. This allows for flexibility in a remote workspace with global team members
- **Benefits:**
  - Clearer Nuanced Communication: Tone of voice and visuals make complex updates easier to understand compared to text-based channels.
  - Saves Time: Meetings are reduced as information can be conveyed efficiently through video.

Case Study 2: GrooveHQ
- **Focus:** Customer support software company.
- **Customer Service:** Their help center includes numerous short, focused explainer videos to supplement text documentation.
- **Benefits:**
  - Improves Self-Service: Customers can often solve issues independently.
  - Visual Clarity: Ideal for showcasing how to use software features or navigate their interface.

Case Study 3: BlendJet
- **Focus:** Portable blenders
- **Origin Story:** Utilizes their founder's personal narrative as a core part of their marketing. Short, energetic videos detail its creation.
- **Benefits:**
  - Authenticity: Customers feel a connection to the real person behind the product.
  - Relatable Struggle: Highlighting the problem their product solves makes it relevant.

Why These Examples Work
- **Solving Real Problems:** Their videos address actual pain points (communication, customer onboarding, etc.)
- **Authenticity:** They don't feel overly polished, aligning with a focus on utility or personal connection.
- **Demonstrating Their Value:** Especially for brands selling services or software, video can showcase the benefits clearly.

5. Getting Started with Video

Overcoming Fear: Acknowledge that getting in front of the camera or tackling editing can be intimidating.

Mindset Shift:

- **Perfection Isn't Required:** Authenticity and offering value are more important than high production quality, especially at the start.
- **It's a Learning Curve:** Emphasize that video, like any skill, improves with practice.

Your First Video:

- **Keep it Simple:** Product demo, customer testimonial, answer one common question, use a basic "talking head" format for a welcome video.
- **Leverage What You Have:** Start with your smartphone and natural light for a budget setup.

Free & Affordable Resources

- **Editing Software:**
    - Mobile: InShot, CapCut, etc., offer easy features for short-form content.
    - Desktop: DaVinci Resolve (free version is robust), OpenShot (open-source option).
- **Royalty-Free Music:**
    - YouTube Audio Library
    - Bensound
    - Incompetech
- **Stock Footage:** If needed, sites like Pexels and Pixabay have free video clips.

Focus on the Fundamentals

- **Clear Audio:** More important than fancy visuals. A cheap lavalier mic makes a big difference.
- **Basic Lighting:** Face a window for natural light, avoid harsh backlighting.
- **Stability:** A phone tripod prevents shaky footage.

Key Takeaways

- **Progress Over Perfection:** Encourage filming that first, slightly awkward, video as the essential step.
- **Iterative Improvement:** Each video teaches you something for the next one.
- **Resourcefulness Matters:** Plenty of tools exist to create impactful videos without a big budget.

Call to Action:

- Brainstorm a few SIMPLE video ideas your readers could implement within the week, based on their business type. Get them excited to take that first step!

Case Study 1: Marques Brownlee (MKBHD)

- **Focus:** Tech reviews and commentary on YouTube. Now one of the largest tech channels in the world.
- **Early Days:** His initial videos were very simple – a webcam, basic edits, and his straightforward review style.
- **Success Factors:**
    - Consistency: Regularly uploaded content, refining his craft over time.
    - Deep Knowledge: His genuine passion for technology shone through.
    - Personality: Developed a friendly, accessible on-camera presence.
- **Takeaway:** Even with minimal gear, his value (expertise and consistent reviews) helped him build a massive audience.

Case Study 2: Tasty

- **Focus:** Short-form recipe videos, primarily for social media.
- **Early Days:** Their now-iconic overhead style was born out of necessity – limited equipment and space.
- **Success Factors:**
    - **Unique Visuals:** The top-down view was novel, making content instantly recognizable.
    - **Accessibility:** Recipes were simple and often used common ingredients.
    - **Trend Aware:** Embraced viral music and editing styles as platforms evolved.
- **Takeaway:** They turned constraints into a strength, proving that a strong concept and catering to audience desires matters more than fancy production

6. Video as a Marketing Must

- **Dominant Format:** Video content accounts for a vast majority of online traffic. Ignoring it means missing out on significant audience engagement.
- **Emotional Connection:** No other medium allows you to convey tone, personality, and complex narratives as effectively as video. Connection breeds loyalty.
- **Meet Audience Expectations:** Users prefer easily digestible visual content. Brands need to adapt to how people consume information.
- **Versatility:** Video works for awareness campaigns, in-depth product demos, building community, and even customer support.
- **The Future is Visual:** With platforms pushing short-form, live, and AR/VR experiences, video will continue to evolve and offer new marketing opportunities.

Call to Action:

- **Start Now, Start Small:** Don't let perfectionism hold you back. Even a simple smartphone video is a valuable first step.

Dive In: AR, VR, and Your Brand

The Next Frontier

AR (Augmented Reality) overlays digital content onto the real world, while VR (Virtual Reality) creates fully simulated environments.

The Potential for Marketing:
- Enhanced Storytelling: Allow customers to interact with brands in new, memorable ways.
- Deepened Connection: Immersive experiences evoke stronger emotions than traditional advertising.
- Bridge Physical and Digital: Create a seamless connection between online and in-store experiences.

Augmented Reality (AR) in Action

- **Accessibility is Key:** Most modern smartphones now have AR capabilities.
- **Types of AR Campaigns:**
  - Virtual Try-Ons: Makeup, clothing, furniture – customers can preview in their own space.
  - Interactive Product Demos: See products in 3D, even manipulate or "take apart" for understanding.
  - Location-Based Experiences: Overlays triggered by reaching specific locations (games, brand-related information).
  - AR Benefits:
    - Reduces Decision Friction: Helps customers visualize purchases, increasing confidence.
    - Boosts Engagement: Gamified experiences or try-ons are simply fun and shareable.

Virtual Reality (VR) Deep Dives

- **Current Limitations:** Headsets are still more niche, but prices are decreasing.
- **Best Use Cases:**
  - **Virtual Showrooms:** Explore a store or products when physically not possible.
  - **Immersive Training:** Simulations for everything from surgery to customer service scenarios.
  - **Experiential Storytelling:** 360° videos or interactive narratives that put the viewer at the center.
- **VR Benefits:**
  - **Access and Scale:** Allows customers to "visit" locations or experience things they otherwise couldn't.
  - **Embodied Learning:** VR is ideal for processes that benefit from a hands-on, experiential approach.

Strategies for Implementation

- **Start with Your Why:** What problem does AR/VR solve for your customers? Don't use it just for gimmick's sake.
- **Accessibility Matters:** If most of your audience won't have headsets, focus on smartphone-driven AR experiences.
- **Integration:** How do AR/VR elements work with your existing marketing channels?
- **Track Success:** Set clear metrics based on your goals (increased try-on conversions, training effectiveness, etc.).

Conclusion: The Future is Immersive

- **Reiterate Potential:** AR/VR transform how customers learn about, interact with, and experience brands.
- **Early Adopters Advantage:** Brands embracing this now position themselves as innovative.
- **Accessibility Will Grow:** As technology improves, these experiences will become mainstream.

Real-world case studies of how brands are effectively utilizing AR and VR for impactful marketing campaigns:

Case Study 1: IKEA

- **Technology:** AR within their mobile app
- **Application:** "IKEA Place" allows users to virtually place true-to-scale 3D furniture models within their own rooms.
- **Benefits:**
  - Reduced Returns: Customers can see if pieces fit and match their style before committing to a purchase.
  - Increased Confidence: Visualization boosts purchase intent, especially for larger investments.
  - User-Friendly: Requires no special equipment, making it widely accessible.

Case Study 2: Lowe's

- **Technology:** Primarily AR, some in-store VR experiences
- **Application:**
  - "Measured by Lowe's" app helps with DIY projects, visualizing measurements, and creating layouts.
  - VR Skill Simulators: Some stores offer VR for training customers on tasks like tiling or flooring.
- **Benefits:**
  - Builds Expertise: Positions Lowe's as helpful, reducing project intimidation for customers.
  - In-Store VR: Creates a memorable experience, differentiating them from competitors.

Case Study 3: TOMS

- **Technology:** VR experience
- **Application:** "Virtual Giving Trip" film let viewers experience a shoe donation trip to Peru in 360°.
- **Benefits:**
  - Emotional Impact: Deeper connection to their mission than standard text or photos could achieve.
  - Shareability: The immersive nature made the campaign stand out on social media.
  - Values Alignment: Attracted consumers who care about social good, strengthening brand image.

Why These Work

- Solve User Problems: They offer genuine utility (better fitting furniture, learning a skill).
- Go Beyond Gimmick: The tech serves the core brand message and customer needs.
- Leverage Strengths: AR's accessibility or VR's immersiveness are used appropriately.

SOCIAL MEDIA PRO MOVES

1. Micro-Communities: Power in the Niche

In 2024, social media is less about broadcasting to the masses and more about cultivating meaningful connections within smaller, hyper-engaged communities. Micro-communities—those tight-knit groups united by a shared passion, interest, or need—are where your brand can truly shine.

Types of Micro-Communities to Consider in 2024:

- **Facebook Groups & Reddit Subreddits:** These continue to thrive, but in 2024, focus on groups that foster active discussion and provide genuine value. Look for moderators who are passionate and maintain a high standard of content.
- **Discord Servers:** Discord is exploding in popularity, especially among Gen Z. Create a server that's more than just marketing; offer exclusive content, host live Q&As, or even gamify engagement.
- **Slack Communities:** While often used for professional networking, don't overlook niche Slack communities that align with your brand. These can be excellent spaces for thought leadership and fostering relationships with industry peers.
- **Emerging Platforms:** Keep an eye on newer platforms like Geneva or Circle, which are specifically designed for building community and fostering meaningful interactions.

Strategies for Engaging with Micro-Communities:

- **Become a Member, Not Just a Marketer:** Don't just drop in to promote your brand. Participate in conversations, offer genuine insights, and build relationships. Become a valued member of the community.
- **User-Generated Content (UGC) Campaigns:** Encourage your community to create content around your brand. This not only amplifies your reach but also deepens engagement and loyalty.
- **Exclusive Offers & Rewards:** Give your community members something special they won't find elsewhere. This could be early access to products, discounts, or unique experiences.
- **Collaborate with Micro-Influencers:** Partner with individuals who have influence within your chosen communities. Their authentic endorsement can be incredibly powerful.
- **Embrace Live Audio & Video:** Host live Q&As, discussions, or workshops within the community. This real-time interaction fosters a sense of connection and intimacy.
- **Co-Create with Your Community:** Involve your community in the development of new products or campaigns. Ask for their feedback, ideas, and insights. This not only makes them feel valued but also helps you create products and messaging that truly resonate.

The Benefits of Engaging with Micro-Communities in 2024:

- **Higher Engagement Rates:** Micro-communities are often more passionate and active than broader audiences.
- **Increased Brand Loyalty:** Authentic connection breeds loyalty and advocacy.
- **Invaluable Customer Insights:** Direct access to your target audience gives you a treasure trove of information to improve your products and messaging.
- **Enhanced Brand Reputation:** Being seen as a valuable contributor to a community can do wonders for your brand's image.

2. Niche Platforms: Targeted by Design

In 2024, social media is less about casting a wide net and more about finding your perfect pond. Niche platforms cater to highly specific interests, demographics, or content formats, offering a more focused audience and a higher chance of resonating with your ideal customers.

Examples of Niche Platforms to Explore in 2024:

- **Pinterest:** Still a powerhouse for visual discovery, Pinterest is increasingly focusing on shoppable content. Leverage its new features like "Idea Pins" for storytelling and the "Shopping List" for driving conversions.
- **Behance:** A hub for creatives, Behance is evolving into a platform for collaboration and community building. Consider hosting live portfolio reviews, Q&As, or workshops to engage with your target audience.
- **Twitch:** Gaming is still king on Twitch, but other categories like music, art, and Just Chatting are on the rise. Explore the possibilities of live streaming events, sponsoring gamers or creators, or even creating your own branded channel.
- **Houzz:** If your brand caters to the home improvement market, Houzz is essential. In 2024, focus on creating high-quality, inspirational content that showcases your expertise and products in real-world settings.
- **Caffeine:** A newer platform focused on live entertainment, Caffeine is a great option for brands looking to connect with a younger audience. Consider hosting live events, sponsoring creators, or even developing your own interactive shows.
- **Clubhouse (and similar audio-based platforms):** While hype has cooled somewhat, Clubhouse and similar platforms still offer a unique space for real-time conversations. Host expert panels, participate in industry discussions, or even create your own branded "clubs" to foster community.
- **The Dots:** This platform caters to the creative community, connecting professionals with job opportunities, inspiration, and networking events. It's a great place to showcase your brand's culture and values.

Strategies for Engaging on Niche Platforms:

- **Content is Still King (But Context is Queen):** Tailor your content to the specific platform and audience. What works on Pinterest won't necessarily work on Twitch.
- **Authenticity is Key:** Avoid overtly promotional content. Focus on providing value, entertainment, or education.
- **Partner with Niche Influencers:** Identify creators who have a dedicated following on your chosen platform and collaborate on campaigns.
- **Community Building is Paramount:** Foster a sense of belonging by hosting events, challenges, or discussions that encourage interaction and connection.
- **Data-Driven Decision Making:** Track your performance on each platform and adjust your strategy accordingly. Don't be afraid to experiment and try new things.

The Benefits of Embracing Niche Platforms in 2024:

- **Higher Relevance:** You're reaching an audience that's already interested in your niche.
- **Lower Competition:** Your message stands out more prominently.
- **Stronger Relationships:** Building community on a niche platform can lead to deeper connections with your target audience.

- **Improved Brand Reputation:** Being seen as a valuable contributor to a niche community can significantly boost your brand's credibility.

By embracing niche platforms, you're not just following a trend; you're carving out a unique space for your brand to thrive. It's about connecting with the right people, in the right places, and in the right ways. It's about building a loyal following that truly resonates with your brand's message and values.

3. Social Commerce Integration

In 2024, social commerce is no longer a novelty; it's a necessity. Consumers expect seamless shopping experiences directly within their favorite social platforms. As a brand, integrating social commerce into your strategy is key to turning casual browsers into loyal customers.

Social Commerce Trends to Watch in 2024:

- **Live Shopping Explodes:** Real-time shopping events, where viewers can purchase products while watching demonstrations and interacting with hosts, are skyrocketing in popularity. Embrace this trend by partnering with influencers or hosting your own live shopping events on platforms like Instagram Live, TikTok LIVE, or YouTube Live.
- **Augmented Reality (AR) Try-Ons:** Allow customers to virtually try on clothes, makeup, or even furniture before they buy. AR is becoming increasingly sophisticated, offering a more immersive and personalized shopping experience.
- **Shoppable Video Content:** Short-form videos on TikTok and Instagram Reels are driving sales like never before. Incorporate product links directly into your videos to make it easy for viewers to buy.
- **Subscription-Based Shopping:** Platforms like Instagram are testing subscription services, allowing brands to offer exclusive content and products to paying subscribers. This can be a great way to build a loyal community and generate recurring revenue.
- **Social Commerce Marketplaces:** Facebook Shops and similar marketplaces are becoming more robust, offering features like personalized recommendations and curated collections. Take advantage of these platforms to expand your reach and streamline the shopping experience.

Best Practices for Social Commerce Integration in 2024:

- **Prioritize High-Quality Visuals:** In the world of social commerce, visuals are everything. Invest in professional photography and video that showcases your products in the best light possible.
- **Make It Easy to Buy:** The fewer clicks it takes to purchase, the better. Simplify the checkout process, offer multiple payment options, and make sure your product descriptions are clear and concise.
- **Leverage User-Generated Content:** Encourage customers to share their purchases on social media. This not only provides social proof but also gives you free marketing.
- **Utilize Influencer Marketing:** Partner with influencers who align with your brand values and aesthetic. Their endorsement can drive significant traffic and sales.
- **Offer Exclusive Deals and Promotions:** Give social media followers a reason to buy by offering special discounts or limited-edition products.
- **Personalize the Shopping Experience:** Use data to tailor product recommendations and offers to individual customers. This increases the likelihood of conversion and fosters a deeper connection with your audience.
- **Build Community:** Social commerce is more than just transactions; it's about building relationships. Engage with your followers, respond to comments and questions promptly, and create a sense of community around your brand.

By embracing these trends and best practices, you can turn your social media presence into a powerful sales engine. In 2024, social commerce is not just an option; it's an essential part of any brand's digital marketing strategy.

Real-life case studies showcasing how brands leverage micro-communities, niche platforms, and social commerce for success:

Case Study 1: Glossier

- Focus: Beauty brand with a minimalist aesthetic and emphasis on community
- Micro-Communities:
    - Early on: Focused heavily on beauty bloggers and micro-influencers in their niche.
    - "Glossier Reps": Brand ambassador program for on-campus promotion and genuine peer-to-peer recommendations.
- Impact:
    - Word-of-mouth: Fostered an authentic, community-driven buzz more effective than traditional ads.
    - User-Generated Content: Fueled their social feeds and drove trust in their products.

Case Study 2: Gymshark

- Focus: Fitness apparel
- Niche Platform: While having a major presence across platforms, they gained early traction on Instagram.
- Strategy:
    - Athlete Sponsorships: Partnering with influential figures within the fitness space.
    - Visual Focus: Their image-driven content was a perfect fit for the platform's strengths.
    - Active Community: Encourages sharing workout photos, #Gymshark hashtags, building belonging.
- Impact: Became synonymous with a fitness lifestyle, not just selling products.

Case Study 3: ColourPop Cosmetics

- Focus: Affordable, trend-focused makeup.
- Social Commerce Integration: Heavily utilize Instagram Shoppable posts.
- Strategy:
    - Collaborations: Frequent limited-edition collections with influencers drives urgency and immediate purchase.
    - Swatch Heavy: Visuals allow direct product comparison which aids quick buying decisions within the app.
- Impact: Shortens the path from inspiration to purchase, capturing impulse buys effectively.

Why These Work

- Audience-Centric: They understand where their target customers are and what kind of content resonates.
- Organic Growth: Strong communities or a presence on niche platforms leads to advocacy and social proof.
- Seamless Experience: Social commerce success relies on making buying as frictionless as possible.

MAKING FRIENDS: SMART PARTNERSHIPS

What if your brand's biggest opportunity for growth isn't found in competition, but in collaboration? Discover how smart partnerships can unlock new levels of success.

1. Co-Branding: Creating Something New Together

In 2024, co-branding is evolving beyond simple logo swaps. It's about creating genuinely new, exciting experiences that resonate with modern consumers. Successful co-branding initiatives tap into shared values, capitalize on complementary strengths, and ultimately deliver something that neither brand could achieve alone.

Types of Co-Branding to Explore in 2024:

- **Product Collaborations:** This classic approach remains powerful. Think limited-edition collections, exclusive product bundles, or entirely new products born from the fusion of two brands' expertise.
    - **Example:** A sustainable fashion brand partnering with a tech company to create a line of smart clothing that tracks fitness and environmental impact.

- **Experiential Marketing:** Co-create immersive pop-up shops, events, or virtual experiences that blend the aesthetics and values of both brands.
    - **Example:** A luxury car brand partnering with a high-end hotel chain to offer exclusive test-drive weekends at stunning destinations.

- **Content Collaborations:** Co-produce a podcast series, a video campaign, or a social media challenge that leverages the unique voices and audiences of each brand.
    - **Example:** A beauty brand teaming up with a mental health advocate to create a series of videos on self-care and confidence-boosting makeup techniques.

- **Purpose-Driven Partnerships:** Align your brand with a cause or social issue that both brands genuinely care about. This can involve co-creating charitable initiatives, donating a portion of proceeds, or raising awareness through joint campaigns.
    - **Example:** A food delivery service partnering with a non-profit organization to combat food insecurity, offering special meal bundles where a portion of the proceeds go to the cause.

Key Elements of Successful Co-Branding in 2024:

- **Shared Values:** The most powerful co-branding initiatives are built on a foundation of shared values and a genuine synergy between the brands. Make sure your missions and target audiences align.
- **Clear Objectives and Roles:** Define what you hope to achieve with the partnership and establish clear roles and responsibilities for each brand. Who's in charge of design? Manufacturing? Marketing?
- **Creative Synergy:** The best co-branding projects result in something truly unique and unexpected. Don't be afraid to push boundaries and experiment with new ideas.

- **Authenticity Above All:** Consumers can spot inauthenticity a mile away. Make sure the partnership feels genuine and natural, not forced or purely transactional.
- **Data-Driven Measurement:** Establish clear metrics for success and track your progress throughout the campaign. Use the data to learn, iterate, and improve future collaborations.

Co-Branding Beyond 2024:

As technology continues to evolve, co-branding will become even more immersive and personalized. Look out for:

- **Virtual Reality (VR) and Augmented Reality (AR) Collaborations:** Brands will create shared virtual spaces or augmented reality experiences that blur the lines between the physical and digital worlds.
- **AI-Powered Co-Creation:** Artificial intelligence will be leveraged to analyze consumer data and generate personalized co-branded product recommendations or experiences.
- **Blockchain-Enabled Co-Branding:** Smart contracts and blockchain technology will streamline co-branding agreements, ensuring transparency and fair compensation for all parties involved.

By embracing these trends and focusing on authenticity, creativity, and shared values, co-branding can be a powerful tool for brands looking to expand their reach, enhance their reputation, and create truly memorable experiences for their customers.

2. Cross-Promotion: Amplifying Your Message Through Collaboration

Cross-promotion, the art of leveraging each other's audiences to amplify your message, is a time-tested strategy that's more relevant than ever in 2024's crowded digital landscape. By strategically partnering with complementary brands, you can reach new audiences, increase brand awareness, and drive engagement without breaking the bank.

Innovative Cross-Promotion Tactics for 2024:

- **Collaborative Social Media Campaigns:** Go beyond simple shoutouts. Co-create engaging content like challenges, contests, or joint live streams that encourage participation and interaction from both audiences.
  - **Example:** Two brands with a shared target audience could launch a TikTok dance challenge featuring a co-branded hashtag.
- **Influencer Takeovers:** Invite an influencer who resonates with both brands to take over each other's social media accounts for a day. This allows you to tap into their followers and showcase your brand's personality in a fresh, engaging way.
- **Joint Events & Webinars:** Co-host virtual or in-person events (if feasible in your region) on topics that are relevant to both brands. This can be a great way to educate your audience, showcase your expertise, and generate leads.
  - **Example:** A fitness brand and a healthy snack company could co-host a webinar on nutrition and exercise.
- **Content Swaps:** Exchange guest blog posts, podcast interviews, or newsletter features. This exposes your brand to a new audience and adds variety to your content calendar.
- **Affiliate Marketing Partnerships:** Promote each other's products or services and earn a commission on each referral. This is a performance-based model, so you only pay when you see results.
- **Bundle Offers & Discounts:** Team up to offer exclusive discounts or bundle deals that incentivize customers to try both brands. This can be especially effective during holiday seasons or special promotions.
- **Cross-Platform Contests & Giveaways:** Leverage the strengths of different platforms by running a contest that encourages followers to engage with both brands across multiple channels. For example, a giveaway on Instagram could require participants to also follow your brand on Twitter or subscribe to your newsletter.

Selecting the Right Cross-Promotion Partners in 2024:

- **Shared Target Audience:** The most successful partnerships are built on a common target audience. Ensure your potential partner's customers are also your ideal customers.
- **Complementary Products or Services:** Ideally, your offerings should complement each other, not directly compete. This creates a win-win scenario where you can cross-promote without cannibalizing each other's sales.
- **Aligned Brand Values:** Partnering with brands that share your values and mission can strengthen your brand image and resonate with your audience.
- **Strong Online Presence:** Look for partners with an active and engaged following on the social media platforms you want to leverage.
- **Open to Collaboration:** Choose partners who are enthusiastic about the partnership and willing to invest time and resources in making it successful.

Measuring Cross-Promotion Success in 2024:

- **Track Website Traffic & Referral Sources:** Use tools like Google Analytics to measure the increase in website traffic from your partner's channels.
- **Monitor Social Media Engagement:** Track increases in followers, likes, shares, and comments on your social media posts that are part of the cross-promotion campaign.
- **Analyze Sales Data:** If you're running affiliate marketing or bundle offers, track the sales that can be attributed to the partnership.
- **Survey Your Customers:** Gather feedback from customers to understand how they discovered your brand and what they think of the partnership.

By approaching cross-promotion with creativity, strategic thinking, and a focus on mutual benefit, you can forge powerful partnerships that amplify your message, expand your reach, and drive meaningful results for both brands involved.

3. Aligning with Shared Values

In 2024, consumers are not just buying products; they're investing in brands that reflect their values. This makes aligning with shared values a powerful strategy for influencer-brand collaborations.

The Importance of Purpose-Driven Partnerships

Today's consumers are increasingly conscious of the environmental and social impact of their purchases. They actively seek out brands that:

- **Take a Stand:** On issues like climate change, diversity & inclusion, mental health, or ethical production.
- **Demonstrate Authenticity:** Consumers can spot inauthentic partnerships. Shared values must be genuinely held by both the influencer and the brand.
- **Drive Tangible Change:** Don't just talk about values; showcase real-world actions and measurable results.

Partnership Ideas for Good (2024 Trends)

1. **Cause-Specific Product Launches:** Co-create limited-edition products or collections where a portion of proceeds goes to a shared cause. This could involve sustainable materials, fair-trade ingredients, or donations tied to specific milestones (e.g., planting trees for every 1000 units sold).

2. **Social Media Challenges with a Purpose:** Launch interactive challenges or campaigns that encourage positive action. For example, a fitness brand and influencer could promote a challenge that donates to a mental health organization for every workout logged.

3. **Influencer-Led Workshops or Events:** Host virtual or in-person events focused on educating and engaging your audience around a shared value. This could be a sustainability workshop, a panel on diversity, or a skills-

sharing session aimed at empowering underserved communities.

4. **Transparent Supply Chain Storytelling:** Collaborate to document and share the story of your product's journey, highlighting ethical sourcing, fair labor practices, and reduced environmental impact. This resonates strongly with consumers who value transparency.
5. **Impact Investing Collaborations:** Partner with organizations that invest in social or environmental projects. This could involve supporting minority-owned businesses, funding clean energy initiatives, or investing in educational programs.

Benefits for Both Brands

- **Enhanced Brand Reputation:** Consumers perceive both brands as more trustworthy, authentic, and committed to making a positive impact.
- **Increased Engagement & Loyalty:** Shared values attract a dedicated community of consumers who are more likely to become long-term customers.
- **Expanded Reach:** By tapping into each other's audiences, both the influencer and the brand can reach new demographics who share their values.
- **Measurable Impact:** Purpose-driven partnerships allow for tracking the social or environmental change you're creating, adding another layer of authenticity to your efforts.

Key Considerations

- **Alignment is Crucial:** Choose partners whose values truly align with your own. Inconsistent messaging will be obvious to consumers.
- **Long-Term Commitment:** The most impactful partnerships are those that evolve and grow over time, demonstrating ongoing dedication to shared values.
- **Measure and Communicate Results:** Track and share the positive impact of your partnership. This reinforces the authenticity of your efforts and inspires further engagement.

Real-life case studies showcasing successful strategic brand partnerships across different models:

Case Study 1: Supreme x Louis Vuitton

- **Type:** Co-Branding
- **Industry:** Streetwear x High Fashion
- **The Collaboration:** Limited-edition collection fusing their iconic aesthetics: Supreme's red logo with Louis Vuitton patterns on bags, clothing, etc.
- **Outcome:**
    - Massive Hype: Lines snaked around blocks, resale prices skyrocketed, cemented Supreme as culturally significant.
    - Expanded Audience: Introduced streetwear fans to luxury, and made LV seem edgier to a younger market.

Case Study 2: Spotify x Starbucks

- **Type:** Cross-Promotion + Integration
- **The Collaboration:**
  - Music in Stores: Starbucks playlists curated on Spotify to enhance ambiance.
  - Rewards: Starbucks loyalty stars earned through Spotify Premium, vice versa.
  - Employee Playlists: Staff-created playlists featured in the Spotify app.
- **Outcome:**
  - Seamless Experience: Blurs the line between physical/digital, enhancing experience for customers of both.
  - Lifestyle Alignment: Positioning both brands as curators of a relaxed, coffeehouse-inspired mood.

Case Study 3: Patagonia x Yerdle

- **Type:** Shared Values (Sustainability)
- **The Collaboration:**
  - "Worn Wear": Patagonia's long-standing used gear resale program expanded via Yerdle's recommerce platform.
  - Messaging: Emphasis on fighting throwaway culture, extending the life of outdoor gear.
- **Outcome:**
  - Reinforces Values: Strengthens Patagonia's commitment to environmentalism in a tangible way.
  - New Audience: Attracts eco-conscious shoppers who may not have initially considered pricier Patagonia gear.

Why These Work

- **Strategic Fit:** The partnerships feel either surprising in a compelling way (Supreme/LV) or naturally aligned with each brand's core offerings.
- **Offer Value:** Customers get something out of the deal – exclusive products, enhanced experiences, a better way to support a cause.
- **Genuine Synergy:** The most successful collaborations leverage what each brand does uniquely well.

PR IN THE DIGITAL AGE

PR has evolved. It's no longer just about getting your brand mentioned in the news. It's about managing your online reputation, creating valuable content, and engaging with your audience on their terms. This chapter explores the new landscape of digital PR and how to leverage it for long-term success.

1. Online Reputation Management (ORM) – The Bedrock of Digital PR

In the digital age, your online reputation is your brand's most valuable asset. Before you pitch stories or seek media coverage, ensure the narrative surrounding your brand is positive and consistent across all platforms. In 2024, ORM is not just about crisis management; it's a proactive strategy for building trust, credibility, and long-term brand value.

Key Areas to Manage in 2024

1. **Search Engine Results Pages (SERPs):**

    - **Dominate the First Page:** Ensure your website, social media profiles, and positive media coverage occupy the top spots for your brand name and relevant keywords.
    - **Optimize for Featured Snippets & Knowledge Panels:** These prominent SERP features can shape a user's first impression.
    - **Showcase:** A fashion brand might partner with micro-influencers to create positive content that ranks well for search terms like "sustainable fashion" or "ethical clothing brands."

2. **Review Sites & Online Communities:**

    - **Active Monitoring & Response:** Track reviews on platforms like Google Business Profile, Yelp, Trustpilot, industry-specific forums, and relevant subreddits.
    - **Engage Authentically:** Thank customers for positive feedback, address concerns promptly and transparently, and showcase your commitment to customer satisfaction.
    - **Showcase:** A tech company could leverage user-generated content (UGC) like unboxing videos or product reviews to build social proof on platforms like YouTube and Reddit.

3. **Social Media Sentiment & Brand Mentions:**

    - **Real-Time Monitoring:** Utilize social listening tools to track brand mentions, trending topics, and potential issues.
    - **Proactive Engagement:** Participate in conversations, answer questions, address concerns, and foster a sense of community around your brand.
    - **Showcase:** A food brand might partner with an influencer known for their positive and engaging online presence to host a live Q&A on social media, addressing any consumer concerns directly and transparently.

2024 ORM Tools & Tactics

- **AI-Powered Sentiment Analysis:** Advanced tools can analyze vast amounts of social media data to gauge brand sentiment with greater accuracy and nuance.
- **Visual Listening:** Monitor not just text, but also images and videos to detect brand mentions and potential issues (e.g., a logo misuse).
- **Personalization at Scale:** Use ORM platforms to automate personalized responses to reviews and comments, while maintaining a human touch.
- **Predictive Analytics:** Leverage AI to identify potential reputational risks before they escalate, allowing for proactive mitigation.

Case Study: Turning a Crisis into an Opportunity

In 2024, a major airline faced a social media backlash due to a customer service incident. Instead of ignoring or downplaying the issue, the airline actively engaged with disgruntled customers, apologized sincerely, offered compensation, and implemented changes to prevent future occurrences. This transparent and proactive approach turned a potential PR disaster into a showcase of their commitment to customer satisfaction, ultimately strengthening their brand reputation.

Key Takeaways for 2024

- **ORM is Ongoing:** It's not a one-time fix, but a continuous process of monitoring, engaging, and building trust.
- **Transparency is Key:** Consumers value authenticity. Own up to mistakes, address concerns head-on, and showcase your efforts to improve.
- **Data-Driven Decisions:** Use ORM tools and analytics to gain insights into customer sentiment, identify trends, and measure the impact of your efforts.
- **Collaboration is Powerful:** Partner with influencers, industry experts, and your own customers to co-create a positive brand narrative online.

2. Crafting a Newsworthy Brand

In 2024, simply having a great product or service isn't enough to capture media attention. To stand out in a crowded digital landscape, your brand needs to be a source of valuable, engaging, and newsworthy stories. This involves shifting your focus from traditional product-centric PR to a more holistic approach that highlights your brand's unique personality, expertise, and impact on the world.

Beyond Product Launches: Finding Your News Angles

Ditch the "new and improved" press release template. Instead, dig deeper and uncover the stories that make your brand truly compelling. Consider these angles:

- **Original Research & Data:** Conduct surveys, analyze industry trends, or gather unique insights that shed light on your niche. Position yourself as a thought leader by sharing data-driven stories that spark conversations and get people thinking.
    - **Showcase:** A fintech startup could conduct a survey on consumer spending habits during economic uncertainty, revealing surprising trends that media outlets would be eager to cover.

- **Thought Leadership & Expertise:** Share your unique perspective on industry challenges, emerging trends, and future predictions. Position your brand as a trusted source of information and insights.
    - **Showcase:** A sustainable fashion brand could publish a thought leadership piece on the environmental impact of fast fashion, offering solutions and advocating for change.

- **Company Culture & Values:** Highlight your company's unique culture, employee stories, philanthropic efforts, or commitment to diversity and inclusion. Humanize your brand and connect with audiences on a deeper level.
    - **Showcase:** A tech company could showcase its innovative remote work culture through a series of employee spotlights, demonstrating their commitment to work-life balance and employee well-being.
- **Social Impact & Sustainability:** Highlight your brand's efforts to make a positive impact on society or the environment. Share stories of your partnerships with non-profits, sustainable practices, or ethical initiatives.
    - **Showcase:** A food delivery service could partner with a local food bank to donate surplus food and create a campaign highlighting their commitment to reducing food waste.

Packaging Your Story for the Digital Age

- **Press Releases 2.0:** Keep them concise, focused, and link to multimedia assets like images, videos, and infographics. Tailor each release to the specific outlet and audience.
- **Visual Storytelling:** Leverage the power of visuals to capture attention and make your stories more shareable. Create eye-catching infographics, compelling videos, or engaging social media posts.
- **Interactive Content:** Explore formats like quizzes, polls, or interactive maps to engage your audience and encourage them to share your content.

Case Study: The Power of Unexpected Angles

In 2024, a small independent bookstore garnered national media attention by launching a campaign to promote literacy in underserved communities. Instead of focusing solely on their products, they positioned themselves as champions of education and social change. This unique angle resonated with journalists and readers alike, generating significant media coverage and boosting the bookstore's reputation as a socially responsible brand.

3. Thought Leadership Content – Building Authority in the Digital Age

Thought leadership content establishes your brand as an authority, not just a seller. In 2024, it's about more than showcasing expertise; it's about sparking meaningful conversations, driving innovation, and fostering a community around your brand's unique perspective.

The Evolving Power of Expertise

Today's consumers are bombarded with information. Thought leadership content cuts through the noise by offering:
- **Credibility & Trust:** Well-researched, insightful content positions your brand as a reliable source.
- **Organic Backlinks & Traffic:** High-quality content naturally attracts links and shares, boosting SEO and visibility.
- **Community Building:** Thought leadership fosters engagement and dialogue, turning customers into advocates.

2024 Formats & Channels for Thought Leadership

Interactive Long-Form Content: Go beyond static blog posts. Explore interactive data visualizations, quizzes, calculators, or multi-part storytelling to immerse your audience.
- **Showcase:** A financial services company could create an interactive calculator that helps users assess their retirement readiness, generating leads and positioning the brand as a helpful resource.

Live & Virtual Events with a Twist: Webinars and online conferences remain popular, but add unique elements like audience polls, expert panels, or gamified challenges to increase engagement.
- **Showcase:** A tech company could host a virtual summit featuring industry leaders discussing the future of AI, incorporating live Q&A sessions and interactive workshops.

Podcast Guesting & Co-Hosting: Reach new audiences by appearing on relevant podcasts or even launching your own branded show with a unique angle.
- **Showcase:** A health and wellness brand could co-host a podcast with a popular fitness influencer, discussing the latest trends in nutrition and exercise.

Opinionated Content & Bold Predictions: Don't shy away from taking a stand on controversial topics or offering bold predictions for the future of your industry. This can spark debate and generate buzz.
- **Showcase:** A sustainable energy company could publish a provocative article on the need for radical policy changes to combat climate change, sparking a wider conversation and positioning the brand as a leader in the field.

Short-Form Video Thought Leadership: Leverage platforms like TikTok and Instagram Reels to share bite-sized insights, quick tips, or behind-the-scenes glimpses into your company's expertise.
- **Showcase:** A fashion brand could create short videos showcasing their design process, highlighting their commitment to sustainable materials and ethical production.

Case Study: Building a Community of Thought Leaders

In 2024, a cybersecurity firm launched a podcast series featuring interviews with leading experts in the field. The podcast quickly gained a loyal following, establishing the company as a thought leader and fostering a community of cybersecurity professionals who actively engaged with the brand's content and services.

Key Takeaways

Focus on Quality & Relevance: Don't just create content for the sake of it. Focus on providing valuable insights that resonate with your target audience.

Experiment with Formats: Don't be afraid to try new things and explore different content formats to see what resonates best with your audience.

Leverage Multiple Channels: Distribute your thought leadership content across various platforms to maximize reach and impact.

Track & Measure: Use analytics to track engagement, measure the impact of your content, and identify areas for improvement.

4. Real-life case studies highlighting effective approaches to modern digital PR:

Case Study 1: Duolingo (Edutainment & Short-Form Video)

- **Focus:** Language-learning app
- **Newsworthy Content:**
  - **Viral TikTok Challenges:** Duolingo's mascot, Duo the Owl, has become a TikTok sensation, starring in quirky and humorous videos that promote language learning. This exemplifies the power of short-form video and edutainment in digital PR.
  - **Creative Brand Collaborations:** Duolingo partnered with popular brands like HBO and Netflix to create language courses based on hit shows like "Game of Thrones" and "Stranger Things." This generated buzz and attracted new users to the app.
- **Outcome:**
  - **Increased Brand Awareness & Downloads:** Duolingo's TikTok success has led to a surge in app downloads and brand recognition.
  - **Positive Brand Sentiment:** The brand's playful and engaging content has resonated with audiences, fostering a loyal and enthusiastic community.

Case Study 2: Patagonia (Purpose-Driven PR & Long-Form Storytelling)

- **Focus:** Outdoor clothing and gear company
- **Newsworthy Content:**
    - **Environmental Activism:** Patagonia has a long history of environmental activism, using its platform to advocate for climate action and sustainable practices.
    - **Long-Form Documentaries:** Patagonia produces high-quality documentaries that tell stories of environmental activism and adventure, further solidifying their brand values.
- **Outcome:**
    - **Strong Brand Loyalty:** Patagonia's unwavering commitment to its values has attracted a loyal customer base that identifies with its mission.
    - **Increased Brand Value:** Patagonia's focus on purpose-driven PR has helped them build a strong brand reputation and increase their overall brand value.

Case Study 3: Gymshark (Influencer Marketing & Community Building)

- **Focus:** Fitness apparel and accessories brand
- **Newsworthy Content:**
    - **Authentic Influencer Partnerships:** Gymshark has built a massive following by partnering with fitness influencers who genuinely align with their brand values.
    - **Community-Driven Content:** The brand actively encourages user-generated content and creates challenges and events that foster a sense of community among its customers.
- **Outcome:**
    - **Exponential Growth:** Gymshark's influencer marketing and community-building efforts have fueled rapid growth and a dedicated customer base.
    - **Global Brand Recognition:** The brand has become a global phenomenon, known for its high-quality products and inspiring message.

Overall, these case studies demonstrate the following key principles of effective digital PR:

- **Audience-Centricity:** Understanding your target audience's interests, values, and preferred platforms is essential for creating impactful PR campaigns.
- **Creativity & Innovation:** Thinking outside the box and experimenting with new formats and channels can help you stand out in a crowded digital landscape.
- **Authenticity & Purpose:** Consumers are drawn to brands that are authentic and purpose-driven. Aligning your PR efforts with your brand's values and mission can build trust and loyalty.
- **Data-Driven Decision Making:** Tracking and analyzing the performance of your PR campaigns can help you identify what's working and what's not, allowing you to refine your strategy and maximize your results.
- **Community Building:** Foster a sense of community around your brand by encouraging user-generated content, hosting events, and engaging with your audience on social media.

By incorporating these principles into your own digital PR strategy, you can increase brand awareness, build trust, and drive meaningful engagement with your target audience.

TRACKING AND FEELING THE VIBES

Beyond surface-level numbers, what's the real story your data is telling you? This chapter goes deeper into the world of social listening, sentiment analysis, and uncovering the emotional resonance of your brand. Learn how to turn data into actionable insights that drive growth and loyalty.

1. The Limits of Vanity Metrics

In the dazzling world of digital marketing, it's easy to be seduced by the siren call of vanity metrics. Likes, shares, follower counts – these numbers flash across our screens, promising instant gratification and a sense of accomplishment. But in the ever-evolving landscape of 2024, these shiny metrics often mask a deeper truth, leading brands astray in their quest to *own the digital space*.

Unmasking the Vanity in 2024

Vanity metrics, while tempting, offer a distorted view of your brand's health. Here's why they fall short in 2024:

- **The Follower Fallacy:** A massive following doesn't guarantee engagement or conversions. Bots, inactive accounts, and purchased followers can artificially inflate numbers, leading you to believe you're reaching a wider audience than you actually are.
- **The Engagement Illusion:** Likes and shares may stroke your ego, but they don't always translate to meaningful interactions or brand loyalty. A post can go viral without driving any tangible business results, leaving you with empty engagement and no real impact.
- **The Traffic Trap:** High website traffic is meaningless if visitors aren't converting into customers or taking desired actions. A poorly designed website, irrelevant content, or misaligned targeting can lead to high bounce rates and wasted resources.
- **The Short-Form Video Vortex:** While platforms like TikTok and Instagram Reels offer immense reach, the focus on short, viral content can distract from building lasting brand awareness and loyalty. Views and likes don't always translate to brand affinity or sales.

The Dangers of Vanity-Driven Marketing

Relying on vanity metrics can lead to:

- **Misguided Strategies:** Chasing likes and shares can distract you from creating truly valuable content that resonates with your target audience and drives meaningful business results.
- **Wasted Resources:** Investing time and money in tactics that boost vanity metrics without considering the bigger picture can lead to a poor return on investment (ROI).
- **Missed Opportunities:** By ignoring more insightful metrics, you miss out on valuable insights into your audience's behavior, preferences, and pain points. This can hinder your ability to tailor your marketing efforts effectively.

Case Study: The Rise and Fall of a Viral Brand

In 2023, a new DTC (direct-to-consumer) brand quickly gained a massive following on Instagram through eye-catching visuals and influencer partnerships. Their follower count skyrocketed, and engagement rates seemed promising. However, when it came to converting those followers into customers, the brand struggled. Their product quality didn't live up to the hype, and their customer service was lacking. As a result, the initial buzz fizzled out, and the brand's growth stagnated.

This cautionary tale highlights the importance of looking beyond vanity metrics and focusing on building a strong foundation of quality products, excellent customer service, and authentic brand values.

Shifting Your Focus in 2024

Instead of chasing vanity, focus on the metrics that matter:

- **Engagement Rate:** Go beyond likes and shares. Measure comments, clicks, saves, and shares to gauge genuine interest and interaction.
- **Conversion Rate:** Track how many website visitors are taking desired actions, such as signing up for your newsletter, downloading a lead magnet, or making a purchase.
- **Customer Lifetime Value (CLTV):** This metric reveals how much revenue a customer generates over their entire relationship with your brand, indicating true loyalty and long-term value.
- **Sentiment Analysis:** Use tools to analyze the emotional tone of online conversations about your brand. Are people expressing positive or negative sentiments? This can provide valuable insights into brand perception and reputation.
- **Share of Voice (SOV):** Assess how your brand's mentions compare to your competitors. This can reveal your brand's visibility and influence within your industry.

By prioritizing these meaningful metrics, you can make data-driven decisions that drive real results and help you truly own your digital space in 2024.

2. Beyond Vanity: Key Metrics That Matter in 2024

While vanity metrics might offer a fleeting sense of accomplishment, they don't provide the actionable insights needed to truly own your digital space in 2024. To navigate the ever-evolving landscape of digital PR, you need to shift your focus to metrics that reveal the true health and impact of your brand.

A. **Engagement Rate: The Pulse of Your Audience**
   - **Why It Matters:** Engagement rate measures how actively your audience interacts with your content. It goes beyond surface-level likes and shares, delving into comments, clicks, saves, and shares—actions that indicate genuine interest and connection. In 2024, fostering meaningful engagement is crucial for building brand loyalty and advocacy.
   - **How to Calculate:** (Total Interactions / Total Followers) x 100
   - **2024 Trend:** With the rise of short-form video platforms like TikTok and Instagram Reels, engagement rate is more critical than ever. It can help you identify which types of content resonate most with your audience and drive meaningful conversations.

B. **Conversion Rate: Turning Visitors into Customers**
   - **Why It Matters:** Conversion rate is the ultimate measure of whether your digital PR efforts are driving the desired actions. It tracks how many website visitors, social media followers, or app users are taking steps towards becoming customers, whether that's signing up for your newsletter, downloading a lead magnet, or making a purchase. In 2024, optimizing your conversion funnel is essential for maximizing ROI.
   - **How to Calculate:** (Number of Conversions / Total Visitors) x 100
   - **2024 Trend:** With the increasing focus on personalization and targeted marketing, conversion rate is becoming a key indicator of how well you're tailoring your messaging and offers to specific audience segments.

C. **Customer Lifetime Value (CLTV): The Long-Term View**
   - **Why It Matters:** While acquiring new customers is important, retaining and nurturing existing ones is even more valuable. CLTV reveals the average revenue a customer generates over their entire relationship with your brand. In 2024, prioritizing customer retention and building long-term relationships is crucial for sustainable growth.
   - **How to Calculate:** (Average Purchase Value) x (Average Purchase Frequency) x (Average Customer Lifespan)
   - **2024 Trend:** With the rise of subscription-based business models and recurring revenue streams, CLTV is becoming an increasingly important metric for measuring brand loyalty and long-term profitability.

D. **Sentiment Analysis: Decoding the Emotional Landscape**
   - **Why It Matters:** In 2024, consumers are more vocal than ever about their opinions and experiences with brands. Sentiment analysis uses AI-powered tools to gauge the overall emotional tone of online conversations about your brand. By understanding how people feel about your brand, you can identify potential issues early on, address concerns proactively, and strengthen your reputation.
   - **How to Measure:** Use social listening tools or sentiment analysis platforms to monitor online conversations and categorize them as positive, negative, or neutral.
   - **2024 Trend:** With the rise of social justice movements and increased consumer awareness of ethical and social issues, sentiment analysis is becoming essential for understanding how your brand's actions and messaging are being perceived by the public.

E. **Share of Voice (SOV): Your Brand's Digital Footprint**
   - **Why It Matters:** SOV measures your brand's visibility and share of conversations compared to your competitors. In 2024, establishing a strong digital presence is crucial for standing out in a crowded marketplace.
   - **How to Measure:** Track your brand mentions across various online channels (social media, news articles, blogs, forums) and compare them to your competitors' mentions.
   - **2024 Trend:** With the rise of niche communities and micro-influencers, SOV is becoming a more nuanced metric. Instead of focusing solely on overall share, it's important to track your SOV within specific segments and communities that are most relevant to your brand.

3. Social Listening: Unlocking the Voice of Your Audience in Real-Time

In the digital age, conversations about your brand are happening constantly, across a multitude of channels. Social listening is your brand's superpower to tap into this vast sea of opinions, emotions, and insights. In 2024 and beyond, it's not just about monitoring mentions; it's about understanding the nuances of sentiment, predicting trends, and proactively engaging with your audience.

Social Listening: Beyond the Buzz

Social listening goes far beyond simply tracking how often your brand is mentioned. It's about:

- **Sentiment Analysis:** Determining whether conversations about your brand are positive, negative, or neutral. This helps you gauge overall brand perception and identify potential issues early on.
- **Topic & Trend Analysis:** Uncovering what topics and trends are associated with your brand, industry, or competitors. This allows you to stay ahead of the curve and tailor your content accordingly.
- **Audience Insights:** Learning about your audience's demographics, interests, pain points, and preferences. This helps you create more targeted and relevant marketing campaigns.
- **Competitive Intelligence:** Tracking what people are saying about your competitors, identifying their strengths and weaknesses, and discovering opportunities for differentiation.
- **Crisis Management:** Detecting early warning signs of negative sentiment or potential crises, allowing you to take proactive measures to mitigate damage.

2024 Trends: Social Listening Evolves

- **AI-Powered Insights:** Advanced AI algorithms are enabling more nuanced sentiment analysis, going beyond simple positive/negative labeling to identify emotions like joy, anger, frustration, or excitement.
- **Visual Listening:** Social listening tools are now capable of analyzing images and videos for brand mentions and sentiment, providing a more comprehensive view of online conversations.
- **Real-Time Response:** With the speed of social media, timely responses are crucial. Social listening platforms are integrating with customer service and community management tools to facilitate quick and effective engagement.
- **Predictive Analytics:** AI-driven predictive models are helping brands anticipate trends, identify potential crises before they escalate, and make proactive decisions based on data-driven insights.

Social Listening Tools for Your Arsenal

- **Brandwatch:** A comprehensive platform with powerful analytics, real-time monitoring, and advanced sentiment analysis capabilities.
- **Talkwalker:** Offers in-depth social listening, competitive intelligence, and image recognition technology.
- **Sprout Social:** A user-friendly platform with robust listening features, social media management tools, and reporting capabilities.
- **Mention:** A versatile tool for monitoring brand mentions, tracking competitors, and analyzing sentiment across various channels.
- **Meltwater:** Provides comprehensive media monitoring, social listening, and influencer marketing solutions.

Beyond the Tools: Human Nuance

While social listening tools provide valuable data, human interpretation is crucial. Understanding the context, nuances, and cultural references in online conversations requires a human touch. By combining the power of technology with human expertise, you can unlock the true potential of social listening and make data-driven decisions that drive real results for your brand.

Real-case studies showcasing how brands effectively employ social listening and sentiment analysis for various business benefits.

1. Starbucks: Turning Complaints into Opportunities

The Challenge: Starbucks faced a surge in negative sentiment on social media due to a perceived decline in customer service quality.

The Solution: Starbucks implemented a comprehensive social listening program to monitor customer complaints and feedback across multiple platforms. They used sentiment analysis to identify key pain points and prioritize areas for improvement.

The Outcome: By addressing customer concerns head-on and making necessary changes to their operations, Starbucks was able to improve customer satisfaction and restore its reputation as a customer-centric brand. They even turned some of their most vocal critics into brand advocates.

Key Trend: Starbucks's success highlights the importance of using social listening to not just monitor sentiment, but to proactively address customer concerns and improve the overall customer experience.

2. Nike: Tapping into Cultural Conversations

The Challenge: Nike wanted to stay relevant and engage with younger audiences who are increasingly interested in social justice and cultural issues.

The Solution: Nike used social listening to identify key cultural conversations and trends that resonated with their target audience. They then developed targeted campaigns that aligned with these values, such as their "Dream Crazy" campaign featuring Colin Kaepernick.

The Outcome: Nike's bold and authentic campaigns sparked widespread discussion and debate, generating significant brand awareness and loyalty among younger consumers.

Key Trend: Nike's approach demonstrates the power of using social listening to tap into cultural moments and create campaigns that resonate with diverse audiences on a deeper level.

3. Netflix: Personalizing the Streaming Experience

The Challenge: With a vast library of content, Netflix faced the challenge of recommending shows and movies that would appeal to individual viewers.

The Solution: Netflix uses social listening and sentiment analysis to track viewer reactions to different genres, actors, and storylines. They then use this data to personalize recommendations, ensuring that users are more likely to find content they'll enjoy.

The Outcome: By delivering personalized recommendations, Netflix has increased viewer engagement and satisfaction, leading to higher retention rates and increased revenue.

Key Trend: Netflix's success highlights the growing importance of personalization in the digital age. By using social listening and sentiment analysis, brands can tailor their offerings to individual preferences, creating a more engaging and satisfying customer experience.

4. Glossier: Building a Community-Driven Brand

The Challenge: Glossier, a beauty brand, wanted to build a loyal community of customers who would actively engage with the brand and advocate for its products.

The Solution: Glossier used social listening to identify and engage with its most passionate fans. They created a dedicated online community where customers could share their experiences, offer feedback, and connect with other Glossier enthusiasts.

The Outcome: Glossier's community-driven approach has fostered a strong sense of brand loyalty and advocacy. Their customers are not just buyers; they're active participants in the brand's story, generating valuable user-generated content and helping to spread the word about Glossier's products.

Key Trend: Glossier's success demonstrates the power of building authentic communities around your brand. By using social listening to identify and engage with your most passionate fans, you can create a powerful network of brand advocates.

Additional Tips for 2024:

- **Embrace Visual Listening:** With the rise of visual content on social media, it's important to track not just text-based mentions but also images and videos.
- **Use AI for Deeper Insights:** AI-powered social listening tools can help you uncover hidden patterns and trends in your data, providing a deeper understanding of your audience.
- **Prioritize Real-Time Engagement:** The speed of social media requires quick responses. Social listening can help you identify and address issues in real time, preventing them from escalating into full-blown crises.
- **Measure Your Impact:** Track the impact of your social listening efforts on key metrics like brand awareness, sentiment, and engagement. This will help you justify your investment and refine your strategy over time.

Real-life case studies that highlight the power of building emotional connections with customers:

A. **Airbnb: "We Accept" Campaign (2023)**

- **The Emotional Hook:** Airbnb launched a campaign celebrating diversity and inclusion, featuring real hosts and guests from various backgrounds, cultures, and identities. The ads emphasized the message that everyone is welcome on Airbnb, regardless of who they are or where they come from.
- **The Result:** The campaign resonated deeply with consumers who valued diversity and belonging. It reinforced Airbnb's commitment to creating a welcoming and inclusive community, fostering a strong emotional connection with its users.

Trend: Brands using their platform to advocate for social change and promote inclusivity.

B. **LEGO: "Rebuild the World" Campaign (2019-Present)**

- **The Emotional Hook:** LEGO's ongoing "Rebuild the World" campaign encourages children to use their creativity and imagination to solve problems and build a better future. The campaign features playful and imaginative ads that inspire children to think outside the box and embrace their unique perspectives.
- **The Result:** The campaign has been highly successful in fostering a sense of wonder and possibility among children and parents alike. It has strengthened LEGO's brand image as a company that values creativity and play, deepening the emotional connection with its audience.

Trend: Brands tapping into nostalgia and playfulness to evoke positive emotions and create lasting memories.

C. **Calm: "Sleep Stories" (2019-Present)**

- **The Emotional Hook:** The meditation app Calm introduced "Sleep Stories," bedtime tales narrated by celebrities and soothing voices, designed to help users relax and fall asleep. The stories cater to a wide range of interests, from nature sounds to fantastical adventures.
- **The Result:** Sleep Stories quickly became a popular feature, with users praising their calming effect and ability to reduce anxiety. The feature has contributed significantly to Calm's growth and solidified its position as a leader in the mindfulness and wellness space.

Trend: Brands addressing mental health and well-being to connect with consumers on a deeper level.

D. **Peloton: Community-Driven Classes (2020-Present)**

- **The Emotional Hook:** Peloton, the interactive fitness platform, fostered a strong sense of community by offering live and on-demand classes led by charismatic instructors who motivate and connect with users on a personal level. The platform also encourages users to share their fitness journeys and support each other through social features.

- **The Result:** Peloton's community-driven approach has been a key factor in its rapid growth and success. The brand has created a loyal following of users who feel connected to each other and to the Peloton brand, leading to high customer retention and engagement.

Trend: Brands building online communities to foster a sense of belonging and connection among their customers.

E. **Microsoft: "We All Win" Campaign (2018)**

- **The Emotional Hook:** Microsoft's "We All Win" campaign featured a heartwarming ad showcasing the company's adaptive Xbox controller, designed for gamers with disabilities. The ad highlighted the joy and inclusivity that gaming can bring to everyone, regardless of their abilities.
- **The Result:** The campaign was met with widespread acclaim for its message of inclusivity and empowerment. It humanized Microsoft and showcased its commitment to making technology accessible to all, fostering a strong emotional connection with consumers who valued diversity and accessibility.

Trend: Brands demonstrating social responsibility and creating products that make a positive impact on people's lives.

These case studies illustrate the diverse ways in which brands can leverage emotional connection to drive engagement, loyalty, and ultimately, business success. By tapping into shared values, experiences, and aspirations, brands can create meaningful and lasting relationships with their customers.

DOING THE RIGHT THING

The digital age has ushered in unprecedented opportunities for businesses to connect with consumers, personalize experiences, and drive growth. However, this era of data-driven marketing and AI-powered tools also comes with a heightened sense of responsibility. Consumers in 2024 are more informed and discerning than ever before, demanding transparency, ethical practices, and a genuine commitment to their well-being.

Increasing Scrutiny:

- **Data Collection Concerns:** The public is increasingly aware of how their personal information is collected, stored, and used. They're demanding greater control over their data and are quick to call out brands that overstep boundaries.
- **Targeted Advertising Backlash:** While personalization can enhance user experiences, consumers are growing wary of invasive tracking and manipulative advertising tactics.
- **Potential for Misuse:** Data breaches, algorithmic bias, and the misuse of AI have fueled concerns about the ethical implications of technology in marketing.

Evolving Regulations:

- **Global Trends:** The European Union's General Data Protection Regulation (GDPR) and laws like the California Consumer Privacy Act (CCPA) are setting a new standard for data protection and consumer rights worldwide.
- **Staying Ahead of the Curve:** Savvy brands are proactively adapting to these regulations, recognizing that they represent the future of ethical marketing practices.

Competitive Advantage:

- **Building Trust:** Ethical brands that prioritize consumer well-being and data privacy will not only avoid legal repercussions but also build trust and loyalty among their customers.
- **Differentiation:** In a crowded marketplace, ethical practices can become a powerful differentiator, attracting conscious consumers who seek brands that align with their values.

1. Privacy Paramount: Safeguarding Trust in a Data-Driven World

Beyond the Bare Minimum

In 2024, simply complying with privacy laws isn't enough. Consumers are demanding more than mere adherence to regulations – they expect brands to genuinely respect their data and prioritize their privacy. The bar has been raised, and companies that fail to meet these elevated expectations risk losing customer trust and loyalty.

The New Privacy Paradigm

This new paradigm is driven by several factors:

- **Heightened Awareness:** Data breaches, privacy scandals, and targeted advertising controversies have made consumers acutely aware of the value of their personal information.
- **Shifting Power Dynamics:** Consumers are no longer passive participants in the data exchange. They want control over their data and are seeking brands that offer transparency and choice.
- **Rise of Privacy-Focused Tools:** The availability of ad-blockers, privacy browsers, and encryption tools has empowered consumers to take control of their online experiences.
- **Regulatory Landscape:** The GDPR and CCPA have established stricter standards for data protection, and similar regulations are emerging worldwide.

Key Areas of Concern

To build trust and thrive in this privacy-conscious environment, brands must address these key concerns:

A. **Data Collection Transparency:**

- **Clear and Concise Disclosures:** Explain in plain language what data you collect, why you need it, and how long you retain it. Avoid legalese and jargon.
- **Purpose Limitation:** Collect only the data necessary for specific, legitimate purposes. Don't overreach and avoid collecting data "just in case."
- **Third-Party Sharing:** Be upfront about whether you share data with third parties, and if so, for what purposes. Obtain explicit consent where required.

B. **User Control and Empowerment:**

- **Granular Privacy Settings:** Allow users to customize their privacy preferences easily. Give them the option to opt-out of specific data collection or sharing practices.
- **Data Deletion Rights:** Honor requests to delete personal data promptly and thoroughly. Make the process simple and accessible.
- **Minimize Defaults:** Avoid pre-selecting options that maximize data collection. Empower users to make informed choices about their privacy.

C. **Data Security as a Priority:**

- **Robust Security Measures:** Invest in encryption, firewalls, and other security technologies to protect customer data from unauthorized access and breaches.
- **Regular Audits and Updates:** Continuously monitor and assess your security practices to identify vulnerabilities and implement improvements.
- **Incident Response Plan:** Have a clear plan in place for responding to data breaches. Communicate transparently with affected individuals and authorities.

Building Trust Through Transparency

Remember, privacy isn't just about legal compliance. It's about building trust with your customers. By prioritizing transparency, user control, and data security, you demonstrate that you value your customers' privacy and are committed to protecting their information. This will not only help you avoid legal and reputational risks but also strengthen your brand image and customer relationships.

Pro Tip: In 2024 and beyond, consider going beyond the minimum requirements. Explore privacy-enhancing technologies like differential privacy or federated learning. Communicate your privacy commitments clearly and proactively to differentiate yourself from competitors and build a loyal customer base.

2. Transparency is the New Black: Honesty as the Ultimate Marketing Strategy

The Perils of Deception

In 2024, consumers are increasingly savvy to "clever" marketing tactics that prioritize short-term gains over long-term trust. Dark patterns (deceptive design elements), manipulative language, and hidden fees can all erode brand reputation and lead to customer backlash.

The Rise of "Authenticity Culture"

Consumers are gravitating towards brands that are authentic, transparent, and genuinely care about their well-being. Social media has amplified the voices of consumers, who are quick to call out brands that engage in shady practices.

Transparency as a Competitive Advantage

Transparency isn't just about avoiding negative consequences – it's a powerful tool for building trust, loyalty, and brand advocacy. Brands that embrace transparency can differentiate themselves in a crowded marketplace and attract conscious consumers who value honesty and integrity.

Key Areas for Transparent Practices

A. **Advertising and Influencer Marketing:**

- **Clear Disclosure:** Ensure that sponsored content, affiliate links, and influencer partnerships are clearly labeled and distinguishable from organic content.
- **Authenticity Over Hype:** Avoid exaggerated claims or misleading language. Focus on genuine benefits and realistic expectations.
- **Paid Reviews:** Disclose any incentives or compensation provided for reviews. Encourage honest feedback, both positive and negative.

B. **Supply Chain and Sustainability:**

- **Ethical Sourcing:** Highlight ethical sourcing practices, fair trade certifications, and efforts to minimize environmental impact.
- **Transparency Reports:** Publish regular reports detailing your sustainability initiatives, progress, and challenges.
- **Traceability:** If possible, allow consumers to trace the origins of your products and understand the manufacturing process.

C. **Crisis Management:**

- **Honesty and Accountability:** In the event of a product recall, safety issue, or other crisis, prioritize honesty and accountability over damage control.
- **Open Communication:** Keep consumers informed about the issue, your response, and steps you're taking to prevent future occurrences.
- **Learn and Improve:** Use the crisis as an opportunity to identify weaknesses and implement changes to prevent similar issues in the future.

Building Trust Through Openness

Transparency isn't just about disclosing information – it's about fostering an open dialogue with your customers. Invite feedback, listen to concerns, and be willing to admit mistakes. By demonstrating a commitment to honesty and accountability, you can build trust that goes beyond transactions and fosters lasting customer relationships.

Pro Tip: In 2024, consider creating a dedicated "Transparency Hub" on your website where you share information about your company's values, practices, and commitments. This can be a powerful way to showcase your commitment to transparency and build trust with your audience.

Remember, in the era of social media and digital scrutiny, transparency is no longer optional – it's essential for long-term success.

3. The Responsible Use of AI and Data: Balancing Power with Principle

The Double-Edged Sword of AI

Artificial intelligence (AI) offers immense potential to revolutionize marketing, from hyper-personalized experiences to predictive analytics. However, the power of AI comes with a responsibility to use it ethically and avoid perpetuating harmful biases or discriminatory practices.

Growing Awareness of AI Bias

In 2024, public awareness of AI bias has reached new heights. Consumers are increasingly concerned about the potential for algorithms to discriminate based on race, gender, age, or other sensitive characteristics. News stories about algorithmic bias in hiring, lending, and criminal justice have raised alarms, leading to calls for greater accountability and transparency in AI development and deployment.

The Ethical Imperative

Brands that embrace AI responsibly can gain a competitive advantage by building trust with consumers and demonstrating a commitment to fairness and equity. Conversely, those that ignore the ethical implications of AI risk damaging their reputation, losing customers, and facing legal challenges.

Areas for Brands to Scrutinize

A. **Data Sets and Training:**

- **Diversity and Representativeness:** Ensure that the data used to train AI models is diverse and representative of the population you serve. Biased data can lead to biased algorithms.
- **Data Provenance:** Understand where your data comes from and how it was collected. Be mindful of potential biases embedded in the data collection process.
- **Data Bias Mitigation:** Implement techniques to identify and mitigate biases in your data sets. Consider using fairness metrics to assess the impact of your algorithms on different groups.

B. **Algorithm Transparency and Explainability:**

- **Understand Your Algorithms:** Make sure you understand how your AI models work and the factors that influence their decisions. This is crucial for identifying and addressing potential biases.
- **Explainable AI:** Strive for explainable AI, where the reasoning behind algorithmic decisions can be understood by humans. This can help build trust and ensure accountability.

- **Regular Audits:** Conduct regular audits of your AI models to assess their performance, identify potential biases, and make necessary adjustments.

C. **Fairness and Equity in Outcomes:**

- **Fairness Metrics:** Monitor fairness metrics to ensure that your AI models are not disproportionately impacting certain groups.
- **Impact Assessment:** Assess the potential societal impact of your AI models before deploying them. Consider potential unintended consequences and take steps to mitigate them.
- **Human Oversight:** Don't rely solely on AI. Incorporate human oversight to review and validate algorithmic decisions, especially in high-stakes situations.

Leading the Way in Responsible AI

By prioritizing fairness, transparency, and accountability in AI development and deployment, brands can demonstrate their commitment to ethical practices. This can lead to increased customer trust, improved brand reputation, and a positive impact on society.

Pro Tip: In 2024, consider establishing an AI ethics board or committee to provide guidance and oversight on AI-related issues. Engage in conversations with stakeholders, including customers, employees, and experts, to ensure that your AI practices align with their expectations and values.

The responsible use of AI is not just a matter of ethics – it's a business imperative. Brands that embrace ethical AI practices will be well-positioned to thrive in a world where consumers demand transparency, fairness, and accountability from the technologies that shape their lives.

FUTURE-PROOFING YOUR BRAND: MARKETING TRENDS TO WATCH IN 2025 & BEYOND

In the fast-paced world of digital marketing, staying ahead of the curve is essential for sustained brand success. What works today might not be as effective tomorrow. This chapter is your crystal ball, offering a glimpse into the key trends expected to shape the marketing landscape in 2025 and beyond. By understanding these shifts, you can adapt your strategies and position your brand for continued growth in the years to come.

1. The Rise of Experiential Marketing: Creating Unforgettable Connections in 2025

Beyond the Transaction: The Experience Economy

In 2025, consumers are increasingly seeking more than just products or services—they crave **meaningful experiences** that resonate with them on an emotional level. This shift towards an "experience economy" is reshaping the marketing landscape, forcing brands to think beyond traditional advertising and focus on creating memorable interactions that leave a lasting impact.

The Next Level of Immersion:

- **The Metaverse: A New Frontier:** The metaverse, a shared virtual space where users can interact with each other and digital objects, is poised to revolutionize experiential marketing. Brands are already experimenting with virtual stores, concerts, and events that offer immersive experiences beyond the physical world.
- **Augmented Reality (AR) Everywhere:** AR is becoming more accessible and integrated into everyday life. Expect to see AR experiences popping up in retail stores, museums, and even on product packaging, allowing consumers to interact with brands in exciting new ways.
- **Sensory Marketing:** Brands are increasingly focusing on stimulating all five senses to create multi-sensory experiences that leave a lasting impression. Think interactive pop-up shops with unique smells, soundscapes, and tactile elements.

Creating Shareable Moments:

- **Gamification and Interactive Content:** Brands are incorporating game-like elements and interactive content into their marketing campaigns to make them more engaging and shareable. Quizzes, challenges, and interactive polls are all effective ways to capture attention and encourage social sharing.
- **Live Events and Experiences:** Live events, whether in-person or virtual, continue to be a powerful way to connect with consumers and create memorable experiences. Brands are experimenting with hybrid events that combine the best of both worlds, offering both physical and virtual participation options.

- **Personalization at Scale:** Thanks to advances in AI and data analytics, brands can now deliver personalized experiences at scale. This means tailoring marketing messages, product recommendations, and even virtual experiences to individual consumers based on their preferences and behaviors.

The Future of Experiential Marketing:

In 2025 and beyond, experiential marketing will become even more sophisticated and integrated into our daily lives. We can expect to see:

- **Hyper-Personalized Experiences:** Brands will use AI to create hyper-personalized experiences that cater to individual preferences and anticipate needs.
- **The Rise of "Phygital" Experiences:** The lines between physical and digital experiences will blur even further, creating seamless and integrated customer journeys.
- **Social Commerce Experiences:** Social media platforms will become major hubs for experiential marketing, offering immersive shopping experiences and interactive product demonstrations.

Key Takeaways:

- Experiential marketing is the future of brand engagement.
- Focus on creating immersive, personalized, and shareable experiences that resonate with your audience.
- Embrace emerging technologies like AR, VR, and the metaverse to create innovative and engaging experiences.

By prioritizing experiential marketing in 2025, brands can create unforgettable connections with consumers that drive loyalty, advocacy, and long-term growth.

2. The Power of Community-Driven Marketing: Unleashing the Voice of Your Tribe in 2025

Beyond Customers: Building a Brand Family

In 2025, savvy brands are recognizing that their customers are more than just buyers – they're a potential community of passionate advocates. Community-driven marketing goes beyond transactions, focusing on fostering genuine connections and belonging among your audience. This approach not only drives loyalty but also creates a self-sustaining ecosystem where your brand becomes a shared passion.

The Evolution of Community:

- **Micro-Communities Thrive:** In 2025, we'll see a rise in smaller, more niche communities centered around specific interests, passions, or identities. These micro-communities offer deeper connections and a stronger sense of belonging than broader, more generic communities.
- **Gamification and Challenges:** Brands are gamifying community engagement with challenges, rewards, and leaderboards to create a sense of fun and competition, encouraging members to participate and contribute.
- **Co-Creation and Collaboration:** Brands are increasingly inviting their communities to participate in product development, content creation, and decision-making processes. This fosters a sense of ownership and investment in the brand.

User-Generated Content (UGC) as Social Proof:

- **Authenticity Reigns Supreme:** In 2025, consumers are increasingly skeptical of traditional advertising and are more likely to trust recommendations from their peers. UGC, in the form of reviews, testimonials, and social media posts, is a powerful form of social proof that can significantly influence purchasing decisions.

- **UGC Campaigns:** Brands are actively encouraging UGC through contests, challenges, and hashtag campaigns. This not only generates authentic content but also deepens community engagement.
- **Influencer Marketing 3.0:** Influencer marketing is shifting towards a more authentic and community-focused approach. Brands are partnering with micro-influencers and brand ambassadors who are genuinely passionate about their products or services and have built strong relationships with their followers.

The Community-Powered Brand:

- **Brand Advocacy:** A strong community becomes a powerful engine for brand advocacy. Loyal community members will organically spread the word about your brand, recommend your products, and defend you against criticism.
- **Customer Insights:** Your community is a valuable source of insights and feedback. Listen to their conversations, understand their needs, and use their input to improve your products and services.
- **Loyalty and Retention:** Community members are more likely to remain loyal to your brand and make repeat purchases. They feel invested in your success and want to see you thrive.

Key Takeaways:

- Invest in building authentic, engaged communities around your brand.
- Leverage the power of UGC to build trust and drive sales.
- Partner with micro-influencers and brand ambassadors who resonate with your target audience.
- Listen to your community, learn from their feedback, and co-create with them.
- Cultivate a sense of belonging and shared purpose among your community members.

By embracing community-driven marketing in 2025, you can unlock a powerful source of brand advocacy, customer insights, and long-term growth.

3. The Evolution of Data-Driven Marketing: Navigating a Privacy-First Landscape in 2025

The Data-Driven Marketing Renaissance

In 2025, data remains the lifeblood of effective marketing strategies, enabling personalized experiences, targeted campaigns, and measurable results. However, the landscape is rapidly evolving, with a greater emphasis on privacy, transparency, and ethical data practices. Brands that can adapt to this new paradigm will unlock unprecedented opportunities to connect with customers on a deeper level while respecting their autonomy.

The Privacy Imperative

- **The Cookie Crumbles:** Third-party cookies, long the cornerstone of online tracking, are facing extinction. Browsers are phasing them out, and stricter regulations are limiting their use. This shift is forcing brands to rethink their data collection strategies and find new ways to understand their customers.
- **Consumer Demand for Control:** Consumers are demanding greater transparency and control over their data. They want to know what information is being collected, how it's being used, and who it's being shared with. Brands that fail to respect these expectations risk losing trust and alienating their audience.
- **The Rise of Privacy Regulations:** Governments worldwide are enacting stricter data privacy laws, such as the GDPR and CCPA. These regulations require businesses to be more transparent about their data practices and give consumers more control over their information.

The Emergence of Zero-Party Data

- **Voluntary Sharing:** Zero-party data is information that consumers willingly and proactively share with brands. This can include preferences, interests, purchase intentions, and lifestyle data.
- **Building Trust:** By collecting zero-party data directly from consumers, brands can build trust and transparency while gaining valuable insights that inform their marketing strategies.
- **Personalization with Consent:** Zero-party data allows brands to deliver highly personalized experiences that are relevant and meaningful to individual consumers, while respecting their privacy preferences.

AI and Machine Learning: The Future of Data Analysis

- **Advanced Analytics:** AI-powered tools are revolutionizing data analysis, enabling brands to uncover hidden patterns, predict consumer behavior, and optimize campaigns in real time.
- **Natural Language Processing (NLP):** NLP enables brands to analyze vast amounts of unstructured data, such as social media posts, customer reviews, and survey responses, to gain insights into sentiment, opinions, and trends.
- **Ethical Considerations:** As AI becomes more sophisticated, ethical considerations become paramount. Brands must ensure that their AI models are fair, transparent, and free from bias.

Key Takeaways:

- **Privacy First:** Prioritize privacy in all your data collection and usage practices. Be transparent, obtain consent, and give consumers control over their data.
- **Zero-Party Data:** Focus on collecting zero-party data directly from consumers to build trust and deliver personalized experiences.
- **AI and ML:** Embrace AI-powered tools to gain deeper insights into your customers and optimize your marketing strategies.
- **Ethical Data Practices:** Ensure your data practices are fair, transparent, and accountable. Avoid using AI in ways that could discriminate or perpetuate harmful biases.

In 2025, data-driven marketing will continue to evolve, with a greater emphasis on privacy, transparency, and ethical data practices. By adapting to this new landscape, brands can build trust with consumers, deliver personalized experiences, and achieve long-term success.

ABOUT THE AUTHOR

With over 20 years of experience in Marketing and branding, in addition to extensive Ecommerce and digital marketing experience, I have honed my skills in crafting and implementing effective strategies to elevate brands in the digital sphere. As an accomplished Ecommerce Marketing professional, I possess a proven track record of successfully devising and executing digital marketing strategies. With adept project management skills, I thrive in dynamic environments while overseeing multiple initiatives simultaneously. My strengths lie in my analytical prowess, clear communication, creativity, interpersonal finesse, and organizational acumen. Whether working independently or collaboratively, I consistently deliver results, fostering a positive and motivating atmosphere to achieve objectives.

www.ingramcontent.com/pod-product-compliance
Lightning Source LLC
Chambersburg PA
CBHW082215220526
45470CB00010B/3175